The Global Underworld

Recent Titles in
International and Comparative Criminology

The Global Underworld: Transnational Crime and the United States
Donald R. Liddick Jr.

All Is Clouded by Desire: Global Banking, Money Laundering, and International
Organized Crime
Alan A. Block and Constance Weaver

The Global Underworld
Transnational Crime and the United States

DONALD R. LIDDICK JR.

International and Comparative Criminology
William J. Chambliss, Series Editor

Westport, Connecticut
London

Library of Congress Cataloging-in-Publication Data

Liddick, Don.
    The global underworld : transnational crime and the United States / Donald R. Liddick Jr.
      p. cm. — (International and comparative criminology, ISSN 1548–4173)
    Includes bibliographical references and index.
    ISBN 0–275–98074–X (alk. paper)
      1. Transnational crime. 2. Organized crime. 3. Organized crime—United
States. 4. Transnational crime—United States—Prevention. I. Title. II. Series.
    HV6252.L43 2004
    364.1′06′0973—dc22   2004044380

British Library Cataloguing in Publication Data is available.

Library of Congress Catalog Card Number: 2004044380
ISBN: 0–275–98074–X
ISSN: 1548–4173

First published in 2004

Praeger Publishers, 88 Post Road West, Westport, CT 06881
An imprint of Greenwood Publishing Group, Inc.
www.praeger.com

Printed in the United States of America

The paper used in this book complies with the
Permanent Paper Standard issued by the National
Information Standards Organization (Z39.48–1984).

10 9 8 7 6 5 4 3 2 1

To my children, Don, Sam, and Mike

Contents

CHAPTER 1

Introduction and Overview

The technological revolution of the twentieth century that produced the integration of world markets and rapid communications and transportation also made possible the proliferation of transnational crime, a pervasive breed of criminality that transcends national boundaries and permeates the globe. While existing for hundreds of years through the commercial activities of European colonial powers, transnational crime expanded rapidly in the latter decades of the twentieth century. It is the province of networks of criminals that flourish in a variety of economic and political situations and in virtually any place where proscribed goods and services are demanded or where oversight of industry, government, and the administration of justice are inadequate. The profits generated from transnational crime and the nexus between "underworld and upper world" criminals shape the course of national and international affairs. Moreover, transnational crime is more often than not *organized crime* and, in its many forms, is responsible for overpriced goods; unsafe products; an unclean environment; the corruption of public officials; the exploitation of women and children for illicit sex; the evasion of income and excise taxes; the poisoning of men, women, and children with harmful drugs; massive thefts and piracy; capital flight from developing nations; and the trafficking in armaments and weapons of mass destruction. The terrorist attacks upon the United States in September 2001 were a manifestation of transnational crime and exemplifies the vulnerability of nations and the terrible impact of this global problem.

The quandary of transnational organized crime is confounded by the fact that the most significant criminals are often political and societal elites—powerful politicians, businesspeople, and informal power brokers. Around

the world, the term "political-criminal nexus" characterizes the most significant forms of transnational crime best.

> A political-criminal nexus, the concentration and fusion of political and criminal
> power, is increasingly reaching the highest levels of many nation-states. Or-
> ganized crime groups develop collaborative relationships with state authori-
> ties to gain access to, and to exploit for their own purposes, the political,
> economic, and social apparatus of the state. To increase the security of their
> operations, they also try to develop arrangements with local and/or national
> political and legal authorities. For their part, state authorities seek cooperative
> relationships with criminal elements for various reasons such as personal ben-
> efits, securing votes, money, or to control enemies.[1]

It is fair in many cases to characterize heads of state and other national
leaders as organized criminals. Treating national resources as if they were
private treasuries, "kleptocratic" rulers siphon national treasuries into their
personal bank accounts. Ferdinand and Imelda Marcos amassed $50 billion
as rulers in the Philippines, and peasant-born Saddam Hussein stole oil wealth
and UN Oil for Food program money to build dozens of palaces. Carlos
Salinas, the former president of Mexico, was forced to flee the country when
his brother was charged with murder and money laundering in connection
with Mexican drug cartels. Even when they are not the holders of high public
office, transnational criminals have become so influential that they have de-
stabilized new democracies in Eastern Europe and the former Soviet Union
and undermined the sovereignty of weak nations in West Africa, the Caribbean, and Latin America.[2] In the United States, law enforcement and congressional investigations have revealed close ties between organized criminals
and the Kennedy, Nixon, Reagan, and Clinton administrations.[3]

A disturbing trend is the development of strategic alliances among
transnational criminals. Drug lords in South America have formed joint ventures with criminal organizations in France and Italy, who have formed alliances with gangsters in Poland and Russia, who have completed the circle
by establishing relations with organized criminals back in Latin America.
German pornographers have established arrangements with Chinese Triads
to make child pornography films in Thailand and Sri Lanka, while American crime networks produce and export "kiddie porn" to countries throughout the European Union. Jamaican "yardies" in England enforce drug rule
in England with automatic weapons provided by the Russian "Mafiya," and
organized criminals from Russia, Poland, and Hungary smuggle children into
Europe to staff that continent's thriving sex market. Serbian gangs transport
young Croatian and Muslim girls to Holland and Germany to work in

brothels.[4] The Czech police have stated that the Sicilian Mafia has signed a deal with Russian crime gangs for trafficking in nuclear materials as well as drugs,[5] while Mexican drug cartels have become partners over U.S. outlaw motorcycle gangs in the methamphetamine and precursor chemicals markets.[6]

The following anecdotes provide a glimpse of the magnitude and scope of the transnational crime phenomenon and its impact upon the United States.

- In August 2002, a Russian man was indicted on sports bribery charges in connection with an international conspiracy to fix figure skating competitions at the 2002 Winter Olympics in Salt Lake City, Utah. The indictment handed down in Manhattan federal court said that Alimzhan Tokhtakhounov, who has been linked to the Russian mob, influenced members of both the Russian and French skating federations.[7]
- The music industry's chief watchdog reported in January 2001 that the industry was losing $5 billion a year due to the pirating of compact discs— transnational crime groups play a major role in this global racket.[8]
- In March 2002, federal authorities unsealed indictments against four individuals, charging them in connection with a kidnapping/murder plot that left five Eastern European immigrants dead in California. The indicted persons were part of a stateside Russian crime group with overseas co-conspirators.[9]
- On October 12, 2002, a terrorist walked into a Bali, Indonesia, nightclub and exploded a bomb, killing more than 180 people. Many of the dead were American tourists specifically targeted by the Islamic militant group Jemaah Islamiyah, a terrorist organization with ties to Usama bin Laden's al-Qaeda network.[10]
- In September 2002, the U.S. Justice Department indicted the leader of the United Self-Defense Forces (AUC), a right-wing terrorist group in Colombia, on charges of transporting seventeen tons of cocaine into the United States and Europe.[11] In November 2002, the Justice Department brought charges against Colombia's left-wing terrorist group (FARC) for kidnapping U.S. citizens and trafficking in drugs.[12]
- In July 2000, U.S. federal agents were still seeking the leader of an Ecstasy trafficking ring with "tentacles throughout the world." Three men had been arrested in connection with a record haul of 2.1 million Ecstasy tablets with a street value of $40 million. Authorities believed that the likely origin of the drugs was the Netherlands.[13]
- In 1998, members of a San Diego street gang were indicted on charges related to the slaying of a Roman Catholic cardinal in Guadalajara, Mexico.

Authorities said that the San Diego gang members were hired by the Arellano Felix drug trafficking organization to assassinate a rival drug king-pin—the cardinal was caught in the crossfire.[14]

- In July 1998, police units in Canada, the United States, Mexico, and Italy arrested twelve people and seized drugs, cash, and jewelry in combined raids code-named "Operation Omerta." The two-year investigation culminated in the dismantling of what was described as one of the world's largest drug smuggling and money laundering operations run by the Sicilian Cuntrera-Caruana family, based in Toronto but with a presence in thirteen countries, including the United States.[15]

- In September 2002, eight members of New York City's Lucchese and Genovese crime families were indicted on charges of extortion, loan-sharking, drug trafficking, and conspiring to transport the proceeds of securities frauds.[16] Earlier in June 2000, sixteen indictments and seven criminal complaints named 120 mobsters, stockbrokers, and Internet start-up executives with strong-arming brokers and manipulating penny stocks—members of all five New York City Cosa Nostra families were named in the securities fraud charges. Prosecutors said that the mobsters bribed or coerced brokers to push worthless stocks, while they used a company called DMN Capital Investments Inc. to infiltrate or control various New York City brokerage firms. Investors were robbed of approximately $50 million in the scams.[17]

- In October 1999, authorities in New York unsealed a three-count indictment against three companies charged with laundering $7 billion through the Bank of New York. The money originated with Russian organized crime.[18]

- In August 2000, U.S. customs officials announced that they had seized $11.4 million in cash from people who were trying to smuggle the money out of the country in everything from cereal boxes to stereo equipment. One international passenger apprehended at JFK Airport in New York City had swallowed forty-six pellets, each containing seven $100 bills.[19]

- In August 2002, U.S. immigration officials announced that they had uncovered the largest child smuggling ring in U.S. history. The smugglers had transported several hundred children at $5,000 a head from El Salvador and Honduras through Guatemala and Mexico and into Los Angeles. The children ranged in age from infancy to the teens, while many were reunited with parents who had also emigrated illegally.[20]

- In December 2001, the United Nation's child welfare agency, UNICEF, described the global child sex trade as a "criminal web worth billions of dollars." UNICEF officials said that 1 million children a year around the world are drawn into prostitution and the modern day slave trade.[21]

- In June 2001, the U.S. Immigration and Naturalization Service (INS), with cooperation from a dozen Latin American and Caribbean countries, arrested 8,000 illegal emigrants from 39 different countries in what was described as the largest ever international alien smuggling operation in the hemisphere.[22]

- In December 1998, American and Canadian officials announced that they broke up an alien smuggling ring that had transported more than 3,600 illegal Chinese migrants into the United States through an Indian reservation in upstate New York. Authorities said that the Chinese ringleaders were assisted by Canadian and U.S. citizens who smuggled the migrants across the St. Lawrence River from Ontario through the St. Regis Mohawk Reservation and into New York City. The operation was described as the largest human smuggling ring ever to penetrate the U.S. northern border.[23]

- The World Wildlife Fund (WWF) released a report in December 2001 that found that the Russian Mafiya controls poaching operations in the Bering Sea that net $4 billion a year. The WWF said that poaching has placed many species at risk of extinction and could contribute to the collapse of entire ecosystems. The Bering Sea fishery produces half of the American and Russian annual fish harvests.[24]

- Westminster police and U.S. customs officials arrested fifteen people and seized an industrial printing press, a shrink-wrap machine, and crates of Windows 95 users manuals from two small print shops in the "Little Saigon" section of Westminster, California. Authorities said that Southern California–based Asian crime gangs produced and sold counterfeit Microsoft products, then used the multimillion dollar profits to finance violent and organized crime endeavors.[25]

- In June 2002, two brothers were convicted for being part of a Lebanon-based Hezbollah cell in Charlotte, North Carolina, that provided material support to the Middle Eastern terrorist organization. Mohamad and Chawki Hammoud, along with some twenty others, helped to finance terrorism by smuggling low-tax cigarettes out of North Carolina.[26]

- In June 2002, government officials confirmed that information about both public and private computer systems that control the U.S. infrastructure was found on computers seized from al-Qaeda, the global terrorist network responsible for the September 2001 terrorist attacks against the United States.[27]

- In 1996, a U.S. government study found that there had been approximately 250,000 attempts to penetrate U.S. Defense computer systems in the previous year.[28]

- In 1994, 1,300 pounds of uranium, originating in Kazakhstan and intended for Saddam Hussein, was successfully intercepted by authorities and is now stored in Tennessee.[29]

Although many of the preceding anecdotes spoke of law enforcement successes, the reality is that transnational crime is a growing threat. Moreover, the response to the transnational crime problem has been tardy and largely ineffective. Although the United Nations coined the term "transnational crime" in the 1970s and President Reagan's Commission on Organized Crime in the mid-1980s devoted hearings and an entire report to Asian organized crime, the recognition of transnational crime as a national security threat was slow to evolve. In February 1996, President Clinton placed an updated National Security Strategy before Congress that for the first time recognized "Fighting International Organized Crime" as a national security issue.

PURPOSE AND OVERVIEW

The purpose of this book is to provide readers with an overview of transnational crime and the impact it has upon the United States. Although important, issues related to definition and theory are not emphasized; rather, the intent is to provide a concise and contemporary description of transnational criminals and their activities that have direct bearing on the United States. The law enforcement and governmental response to the problem, both within the United States and internationally, will also be explored. In the end, I hope this book will serve to educate general readers, scholars, students, law enforcement professionals, and others of the scope, magnitude, and nature of the problem.

Although the perpetration of crime across national boundaries may involve the actions of individuals and the coordinated ventures of loose networks of people, it is also true that there are identifiable criminal entities in the United States that are best characterized as transnational organized crime groups. Chapter 2 will provide a description and overview of the structure and activities of these groups, which are of two types: (1) organized crime groups of foreign origin or that are based in foreign lands but maintain a significant presence in the United States, and (2) "homegrown" organized crime groups whose range of activities extend beyond U.S. borders. Domestic organized crime and terrorist groups without transnational dimensions are not included. Transnational terrorist organizations in the United States and affecting U.S. interests are covered in Chapter 5.

The most significant and long-lasting domestic organized crime group with international scope is the American Cosa Nostra. An overview of transnational crime groups in the United States would be remiss without describing the structure and illicit activities of this conglomerate of crime "families." The other major homegrown groups in the United States are outlaw motorcycle gangs (for example, the Hell's Angels and the Pagans). Foreign-based crime organizations to be detailed include the Russian Mafiya, Chinese Triads, Jamaican Posses, Mexican and Colombian drug "cartels," the Japanese Yakuza, the Sicilian La Cosa Nostra, and Nigerian drug traffickers.

Because of its geographic proximity, Canada's problem with transnational organized crime will also be described in this chapter.

Perhaps the most pervasive of all transnational criminal enterprises is the global narcotics trade. The prohibition of some drugs in the United States has created huge black markets that contribute to competitive violence among street gangs, the corruption of public officials, an overburdened criminal justice system, and the growth of criminal syndicates. In recent years, the success in weakening the Colombian Medellin cocaine cartel has merely contributed to the rise of the Cali cartel as well as Mexican traffickers. The Mexican cartels control the supply of 70 percent of the cocaine consumed in the United States, 80 percent of the foreign-grown marijuana, and 80 percent of the raw methamphetamine ingredients.[30] Colombian crime groups have taken over the U.S. heroin market from Asia, moving a nearly 100 percent pure product through their previously established Caribbean cocaine routes.[31]

The illicit traffic in armaments is highly lucrative and is intimately linked to the global drug trade. The Ninth United Nations Congress on the Prevention of Crime and the Treatment of Offenders stated in a recent report that transnational organized crime is involved in the illegal arms trade and subversive activities that tamper with the rule of law in different parts of the world. Drugs for weapons deals have become common, while many ethnic and political conflicts are worsened by the illicit drugs and arms connection. Weapons trafficking is complicated by the fact that the distinction between the legal and illegal supply of arms is not always clear. Transactions that may have been legal initially nevertheless circumvent the law because the end user is either a "rogue state that the international community is trying to isolate" or an ethnic group attempting to circumvent an arms embargo.[32] In some cases, illegal arms trafficking has been sanctioned by nations.[33]

Smuggling and trafficking contraband across international borders is intimately linked to organized transnational theft. The hijacking of trucks, cargo theft from airport terminals, and piracy on the high seas are contemporary transnational crime problems.[34] Automobile theft is a multibillion dollar industry with established international dimensions. A 1996 congressional committee detailed how vehicles are stolen in the United States and shipped out of the country in shipping containers aboard cargo ships. Vehicles swiped in New York City, for example, sell for three times their American value in the Russian republics.[35] Art and antiquities theft, software piracy, and the theft of computers and computer components are common. (CPUs are worth more money by weight than drugs and are used as currency in certain parts of Mexico.)[36]

Trafficking in people has several transnational criminal dimensions, including illegal migrations, the smuggling of women and children for the purposes of prostitution and pornography, and the trade in human body organs. Authorities believe that criminal organizations are smuggling 1 million people a year, an illicit business that yields untold billions. Trafficking in women and children for the purpose of prostitution is closely linked to illegal migrant trafficking. In fact, an insidious relationship exists between the demand for smuggling services and the need for laborers in the commercial sex industry. While many migrants are transferred to foreign lands with the full knowledge that they are to work as prostitutes, other highly vulnerable people indebted to smugglers are forced into sexual slavery.[37]

The export of toxic wastes to developing countries and a huge black market in ozone-depleting substances emerged as transnational criminal enterprises in the 1980s and 1990s. The combination of liberalized international trade policies and the rising cost of legal disposal in rich industrialized nations has created this growing trade in hazardous wastes. Initiatives like the Basel Convention failed to stop the export of toxins to the third world, but did precipitate a significant black market in waste exports. The illegal traffic in chlorofluorocarbons (CFCs) expanded after the implementation of the Montreal Protocol's production and consumption control rules. Loss of tax revenue generated swift action in the United States, where an interagency task force confiscated 500 tons of illegal CFCs and recovered $40 million in lost tax revenues in its first year (1994).[38] Also in the category of "eco-crimes" is the illegal trade in exotic plants and animals, a huge global industry. In 1996, authorities estimated that between $10 and $20 billion in exotic life forms were traded illegally, with the United States leading the list of buyers.[39] Chapter 3 will cover these areas and the ways in which they overlap.

Chapter 4 discusses the world of money laundering and other financial crimes. In the first International Crime Threat Assessment published by the Clinton White House in December 2000, a plethora of financial crimes was identified as adversely affecting U.S. companies and the U.S. economy. Activities identified in the assessment included economic trade crimes such as piracy, the violation of intellectual property rights through product piracy and counterfeiting, industrial theft and economic espionage, counterfeiting U.S. currency and other monetary instruments, sophisticated fraud schemes directed at individuals and businesses, high-tech computer crimes targeting businesses and financial institutions, and money laundering.[40]

Money laundering in particular is an activity that blurs the distinction between organized crime and white-collar crime, as the transfer, concealment, repatriation, and reinvestment of transnational criminal profits is dependent on powerful world bankers in collusion with a shady assortment of criminal entrepreneurs, lawyers, politicians, and members of the intelligence community. Officials in tax-haven countries such as Switzerland, Hong Kong, and Luxembourg too often welcome the absorption of dirty money into their banking systems, where the money is hidden from investigators by bank secrecy laws. Money laundering is the activity that ensures the wheels of transnational organized crime will continue to turn. Moreover, the ability to transfer funds around the globe endlessly and with great velocity makes it extremely difficult if not impossible for investigators to trace the flow of cash (even if they had the resources to pursue even a fraction of the larger transactions).[41]

Chapter 5 turns to terrorism and weapons of mass destruction. The destructive impact of transnational crime was brought home to the United States on September 11, 2001, when nineteen Islamic terrorists of the al-Qaeda group hijacked four passenger jets and flew them into the World Trade Center towers in New York City, the Pentagon building in Washington, D.C., and a field in southwestern Pennsylvania, killing 3,000 people. In addition to al-Qaeda, which is thought to have as many as 5,000 operatives within the United States, various Islamic terrorist groups threaten U.S. interests and allies throughout the world—the Abu Sayyaf in the Philippines, Hamas, the PLO, Hezbollah in the Middle East, and Jemaah Islamiyah in Indonesia all have transnational range and directly menace the United States. Moreover, a number of regimes finance and actively promote terrorism: The 2001 State Department list of state sponsors of terrorism included Iraq, Iran, Cuba, North Korea, Libya, Syria, and Sudan.[42]

One of the more frightening aspects of international terrorism is the illicit traffic in nuclear materials, as well as the potential use of chemical (sarin

gas, for example) and biological agents (for example, anthrax and smallpox)
to kill thousands of people in a single attack. The Russian Mafiya are prominent in the theft of nuclear materials, as are former Red Army soldiers, former
KGB agents, ex-officers of the Stasi (the East German secret service),
German-based Russian mafiya gangs, South African groups, the Italian Mafia,
and the Serbian mafia. These transnational criminals transport nuclear materials out of the former Soviet Republics through Eastern Europe, into
Germany, and on to clients in Libya, Iraq, Iran, Algeria, and Pakistan. Authorities have documented hundreds of incidents of smuggling or attempted
smuggling of nuclear materials.[43]

A recent trend in the realm of terrorism is commonly referred to as
cyberterrorism. The revolution in computer and information technology and
global communications has also placed vital U.S. systems in danger of attack from computer hackers. National defense and control systems for nuclear
weapons, power grids, aircraft control, banking and trade, and the computer
systems of private corporations are all at risk. Author Walter Laqueur has
suggested that with $1 billion and twenty hackers a single terrorist could
"shut down" the United States.[44]

Given the broad scope and significance of transnational crime, no discussion would be complete without an examination of responses to it. Chapter
6 turns to that subject. The problem of transnational crime was not addressed
in a meaningful way until the 1990s. In the United States, the Committee
on Foreign Affairs in the House of Representatives and the House's Committee on International Relations held hearings on the threat of inter-
national/global organized crime in November 1993 and January 1996
(respectively).[45] On October 21, 1995, President Clinton issued Presidential Decision Directive 42 (PDD-42), ordering agencies of the executive
branch of the U.S. government to devote additional resources and work more
closely with other governments to develop a global response to the threat
of international crime. The outgrowth of PDD-42 was the first U.S. International Crime Control Strategy (ICCS) published in May 1998. The ICCS
detailed a plan of action to launch a sustained and long-term attack on
transnational crime, framed by eight broad goals: extend the first line of
defense beyond U.S. borders, protect U.S. borders by attacking smuggling
and smuggling-related crimes, deny safe haven to international criminals,
counter international financial crime, prevent criminal exploitation of international trade, respond to emerging international crime threats, foster international cooperation and the rule of law, and optimize the full range of
U.S. efforts.[46] In the closing months of the Clinton administration, the U.S.
government's first comprehensive statement about global organized crime,

the International Crime Threat Assessment, was made available to the public. Also in 2000, the United Nations approved the Palermo Convention on Transnational Crime.[47]

Chapter 6 will also examine in detail specific U.S. legislative initiatives meant to combat transnational crime. The discussion will include, but not be limited to, significant laws such as the Money Laundering Control Act (1986), the Organized Crime Control Act (1970), the Racketeer Influenced and Corrupt Organizations statute (RICO) (1970), and in response to the terrorist attacks in 2001, the Patriot Act (2001) and the Homeland Security Act (2002). Other law enforcement tools to be examined include the use of electronic surveillance and asset forfeiture. Special attention will be paid to technological advances, such as the use of satellites to track people and shipping containers, biometric identifiers, and encryption technology.

DEFINITION AND CONCEPTUALIZATION

Although this book will not be overly concerned with definition, conceptualization, and theory (focusing instead on contemporary descriptions and accounts), the examination of these issues in relation to the term "transnational organized crime" is obligatory. Although transnational organized crime is not a new phenomenon, the phrase used to describe these activities is a recent development in the criminological lexicon. The United Nations Crime Prevention and Criminal Justice Branch first coined the term itself in 1975 in an attempt to identify criminal acts that transcend international boundaries, transgress the laws of several states, or have an impact on another country.[48] In 1994, the secretariat of the UN sought to assess the prevalence of transnational crime through the *Fourth United Nations Survey of Crime Trends and Operations of Criminal Justice Systems*. At that time, the UN defined transnational crime as "offences whose inception, prevention, and/or direct or indirect effects involved more than one country."[49] The secretariat also identified eighteen categories of transnational crime:

> . . . money laundering, illicit drug trafficking, corruption and bribery of public officials, infiltration of legal business, fraudulent bankruptcy, insurance fraud, computer crime, theft of intellectual property, illicit traffic in arms, terrorist activities, aircraft hijacking, sea piracy, hijacking on land, trafficking in persons, trade in human body parts, theft of art and cultural objects, environmental crimes, and other offenses committed by organized criminal groups.[50]

"Transnational crime" is not a legal or juridical term, but a criminological one. Identified transnational crimes are defined differently from one nation to the next, yet all have the common characteristic of transcending the jurisdiction of any given state. Moreover, while transnational crimes may be committed by individuals, observations from around the world invariably reveal that transnational crime is also organized crime. Finally, transnational organized crime, in its most pervasive and damaging forms, typically involves what many criminologists now refer to as a "political-criminal nexus."[51]

Several useful paradigms exist that can help explain the various manifestations of transnational criminal networks. One such perspective is called the "stage-evolutionary model," which sees criminal groups as evolving from one stage or form to more advanced stages. The model includes "predatory," "parasitical," and "symbiotic" stages. At the predatory stage, the criminal group is essentially a street gang or group confined to a relatively narrow area, such as a neighborhood. At this stage, violence is used as a defense, to control a territory, to eliminate enemies, and to create a monopoly over the illicit use of force. Long-range activities and planning are usually absent, but once the criminal group gains recognition among "legitimate power brokers," local politicians and community businessmen use the gang's skill at interpersonal violence to get out the vote, collect debts, and coerce or eliminate political and business rivals.[52]

At the predatory stage, the criminal gang is subservient to political and economic community actors and is typically controlled by them through law enforcement agencies. Once criminal gangs develop a corrupt relationship with "legitimate power sectors," they emerge from the predatory stage into the parasitical stage. Opportunities arising from the establishment of black markets (as with alcohol prohibition in the United States in the 1920s and 1930s) and the breakdown of civil society (as in the Balkans in the 1990s) provide the impetus for the movement of the predatory criminal gang into a full-fledged parasitical organized crime group. Parasitical crime groups feed off society by providing demanded illegal goods and services, with underworld and upper-world society bound together through political corruption. At the parasitical stage, organized crime groups amass resources and extend their networks into the legitimate economic sectors of society. Now organized crime has become more of an equal to the state, as opposed to a servant.[53]

Finally, at the symbiotic stage, the link between organized crime and political systems evolves into a mutually beneficial exchange relationship. In this final most advanced stage, the state apparatus actually becomes dependent on the former parasite and its monopolies and networks. The forty-year relationship between the Christian Democrats and the Mafia in Italy, the symbiotic ties among the Japanese government and the Yakuza, and the influence of cocaine cartels over Colombia's legislative and judicial systems are prime examples of the final and most damaging phase of organized crime development. When organized criminal groups advance to the symbiotic stage (and to a lesser extent, perhaps, the parasitical stage), transnational criminal networks often develop.[54]

Another useful way of viewing the problem of transnational organized crime is as complex networks of patron-client relationships. This perspective stresses the importance of personal and interpersonal relations, quasi-groups, networks, and power relations.[55] From the patron-client viewpoint, the shape of illegal markets and the manner in which illegal goods and services are provided is determined by groups or "quasi-groups" of individuals who channel the flow of societal resources (including revenue derived from criminal enterprises). In its simplest form, a patron-client relationship may be defined as "an alliance between two persons, of unequal status, power or resources each of whom finds it useful to have as an ally someone superior or inferior to himself." The superior member of such an alliance is called the patron and the person with less power, the client. Schmidt adds:

> In these relationships patrons and clients are in many ways dependent on each other. Each party at any time can supply the other with something that they cannot normally obtain on their own. In most circumstances, the favors that patrons do for their clients are material, while clients usually provide to their patron the expenditure of labor or effort. Asymmetry in patron-client relationships is seen as resulting from the unequal distribution of chances (potential of power, prestige, and wealth) among societal participants.[56]

Scholars such as Joseph Albini, Anton Blok, Alan Block, Henner Hess, and Pino Arlachi have found the patron-client relations perspective specifically well suited to an analysis of organized crime. Block, for example, describes organized crime as being "formulated through patron-client cliques and coalitions," and defines it as "a system composed of under- and upper-world individuals in complicated relations of reciprocity."[57] Blok, Hess, and Arlachi applied the notion of patronage and clientelism to the appearance of the mafiosi in post-feudal Sicily.[58] Joseph Albini has resisted the idea that organized crime is a rigid, formally structured organization, but has instead developed the notion of patronage systems. Albini observed that powerful individuals in syndicate crime do not exercise equal power, and therefore patron-client relationships develop between syndicate functionaries and "legitimate society," and among syndicate members themselves. As such, syndicate enterprises are characterized as being very fluid and changeable, while criminal networks comprise loosely structured and informal relationships.[59]

Because transnational organized crime often involves what has been called the "political-criminal nexus," a major strength of the patron-client relations perspective is obvious. Typical conceptualizations of organized crime see public officials and powerful private entities as being peripheral to actual criminal organizations—politicians are "corrupted," and businesses are "infiltrated." In short, the role played by the most significant players in organized crime is characterized as passive. From a patron-client viewpoint, no distinction is made between criminals on the street selling illegal goods and services and criminals in city hall pocketing their share and deciding generally how resources will be distributed. Public officials and private entrepreneurs are not perceived as being peripheral to criminal organizations, but are recognized as active participants in the processes that organize crime.

A Classification Scheme

Aside from providing a definition and some theoretical frameworks that help explain the phenomenon, it may also be useful to provide a typology of transnational organized crime. Peter Lupsha has done so, constructing a classification scheme "along a continuum based on the degree of symbiotic consolidation and incorporation into the culture of the nation-state in which groups are rooted."[60] Lupsha's description of transnational crime group types follows:

> First, there are groups that are structurally and symbolically deeply embedded within the political and economic systems of a nation. In these situations, transnational organized crime has such vast capital resources and skills reserves and systemic penetrations that, should they choose, or be forced to, they can confront the nation-state as equals, or within geographic regions or specific economic sectors or industries, or in weak, failed or troubled states, as superiors. These groups, I would label, "Consolidated or Corporatized."
>
> A second set of transnational organized crime groups have a number of symbiotic ties to the state, yet at the same time frequently appear to be subject to the will and power structures of the state. In many senses they appear to be employees or franchised by dominant state institutions (police, military, interior, intelligence, judicial) which use them to their ends and taxes them remorselessly. Countries where this pattern appears to occur include Taiwan, Mexico, the Peoples Republic of China, Nigeria, Pakistan, Syria, Lebanon, and at times, Israel. These groups I would label as "Transitional or Linked organizations."
>
> A third set of transnational organized crime groups I call "In-Flux: Emergent." These are groups which have either emerged out of the absence of civil society, as in the former Soviet Union and Eastern Europe, or, out of insur-

gency and conflict, as in Sri Lanka, Burma, Afghanistan, India, Turkey, and elsewhere, or out of both sets of conditions. Often these organized criminal groups are linked prior institutions of the state, such as the old organs of intelligence, the military of former totalitarian bureaucracy and economy.[61]

Having defined and examined the scope of the problem, let us now turn to a description of transnational crime groups operating in and influencing the United States.

CHAPTER 2

Principal Transnational Crime Groups Affecting the United States and Canada

This chapter will describe and detail the activities of transnational crime groups impacting the United States and Canada. Some groups, such as the American Cosa Nostra and outlaw motorcycle gangs, are indigenous to the United States, but have become so expansive that they are transnational in their range. Other criminal organizations, like the Russian Mafiya, the Japanese Yakuza, and the South American drug cartels are foreign-based but maintain a significant presence in and influence the United States through their transnational criminal enterprises. Because of its geographical and economic proximity, an overview of Canada's organized crime problem is examined here as well. Not included here are many organized criminals and crime groups that are limited in scope to just one country or region—some of these entities, such as American prison gangs and American youth street gangs, may nevertheless comprise a significant segment of organized crime activity in the United States.

Due to the American Cosa Nostra's historical significance and the fact that it still maintains a major presence despite tremendous law enforcement opposition, the overview will begin with a look at it.

LA COSA NOSTRA

Italian-American organized criminals have operated in the United States since the 1880s, when the first significant wave of Italian emigration to America began. Popularly known as the "Mafia" (from the Sicilian word *Mafioso*, or "man of honor"), bands of Sicilian career criminals provided illegal goods and services and perpetrated crimes of extortion in cities like New

York, Philadelphia, New Orleans, and San Francisco well before the turn of
the twentieth century. Enriched by the huge black market booze industry
in the 1920s and driven by a desire to transcend old-style Sicilian management, which limited criminal partnerships with non-Italian racketeers, infamous gangsters like Charles "Lucky" Luciano and Meyer Lansky engineered
a consolidation of sorts that gave birth to what is now known as La Cosa
Nostra, or "Our Thing." Comprising two dozen crime "families" spread
throughout the United States and regulated to some extent by a small body
of the most powerful crime bosses (called the "Commission"), La Cosa
Nostra has been, since the 1930s, the most significant network of organized
crime groups in the United States.[1]

By the time of the televised congressional Kefauver Committee hearings
in 1951, the government, the law enforcement community, the media, and
the general public increasingly viewed organized crime as synonymous with
Italian-American organized crime families.[2] The infamous meeting of organized criminals in Appalachin, New York, in 1957 fueled the idea that the
Mafia was national in scope and very well organized, while the testimony of
the infamous mob turncoat Joseph Valachi formed the basis for the conclu-
sions of President Lyndon Johnson's Task Force Report on Organized Crime
in 1967. Johnson's task force concluded that organized crime was virtually
synonymous with Cosa Nostra, a national corporate-like crime organization
composed of Italian-Americans.[3]

While some in academia, government/law enforcement, and the media
have incorrectly attributed to La Cosa Nostra corporate-like (nothing so
formal exists), national (the influence of Cosa Nostra families, while extensive and even transnational, tends to be regional), and monolithic features
(the various Italian crime "families" are separate and distinct entities), the
confederation of Italian-American crime organizations are nevertheless quite
remarkable in their durability and longevity. Due in large part to its ability
to compromise government officials and institutions and instill fear in those
who would dismantle it, La Cosa Nostra's tenacity is principally a function
of effective management and the maintenance of authority. Each "family"
possesses a hierarchical authority structure, with a "boss" at the top, an
"underboss" to act as a buffer and to channel communications, a consigliere
(counselor) to mediate disputes and to advise the boss, and several capos or
captains, each of whom manages his own unit of "soldati" or "street soldiers"
who comprise the bottom of the pyramid. Given that each capo operates with
considerable autonomy, that individual families are separated by geography
and the need to conceal their activities, and that law enforcement effort ar-
rayed against them has been prodigious, the survival of La Cosa Nostra into

the twenty-first century must be viewed as staggeringly impressive. In addition to continued demand for illicit products and services, "Our Thing" persists due to southern Italian cultural traditions assimilated by Italian criminals into their organizational milieu: loyalty to the group before family, god, or country; complete obedience to ranking members; a system of mutual obligations (such as providing for police protection in return for a specified cut of illicit proceeds); and, of course, "omerta"—the code of silence.[4]

Rapid transportation, space-age communications, and the expeditious management of information have had a significant impact on the nature of Cosa Nostra. Although the law enforcement community has employed new and better techniques in their fight against organized criminals, illegal entrepreneurs have countered with increasingly sophisticated methods and an expansion of their illicit activities. From the illegal disposal of hazardous waste to the laundering of illicit profits through commercial banks to fuel-related tax scams, the American "mafia" has evolved and expanded the scope of its activities.

The activities of the American Cosa Nostra have been unbounded and intertwined with legitimate commerce. Racketeering in business and labor is a prime example. Whether by extortion or through legal ownership, organized criminal elements continue to impact American business and commerce in profound ways. The racketeers' legacy in labor and business is the systematic restraint of trade, the pillaging of union benefit funds, and the laundering of illicit revenue through otherwise legitimate business and financial institutions. A partial list of legitimate industries infiltrated by Cosa Nostra elements include advertising, appliances, automobiles, banking, coal, construction, pharmaceuticals, electrical equipment, florists, meat, seafood, dairy products, groceries, cheese, olive oil, fruit, garments, import-export businesses, insurance, liquor, news services, newspapers, oil, paper products, radio, ranching, real estate, restaurants, scrap metal, shipping, steel, television, theaters, and transportation. It seems that the list of possibilities is bounded only by opportunity.[5] In 1979, the U.S. Justice Department estimated that Cosa Nostra members owned 10,000 legitimate businesses that generated approximately $12 billion annually.[6]

The racketeering side of Cosa Nostra activities has involved the creation and control of employer trade associations and the infiltration of labor unions. Modern racketeers, in concert with government officials, have infiltrated numerous industrial sectors and overwhelmed the regulatory role of the government, most notably in those economic zones involving the protection of the environment, the shipment of goods (especially trucking), and the construction of buildings.[7] New York City's construction industry exemplifies the scope of Cosa Nostra's power, where for some years any major project was subject to a 2 percent "tax" by organized criminals. In the prodigious realm of health care, Cosa Nostra families have looted some of the nation's largest union health and welfare funds through fraudulent health care plans.[8]

Industrial and labor racketeering is, of course, only one segment of Cosa Nostra's role in the modern American political economy. While the advancing technological base has brought about higher standards of living and made possible the enhanced pursuit of leisure activities, the proliferation of businesses catering to human pleasures has been tightly regulated by the state, thus creating the perfect formula for large-scale and organized vice activities—primarily gambling, prostitution, pornography, and drugs.

Cosa Nostra groups have generated tremendous profits through their hidden ownership of legal casinos in Las Vegas and Atlantic City. Front men for mobsters were given huge pension fund loans from the International Brotherhood of Teamsters in order to acquire Las Vegas casinos, which were systematically looted through "skimming" operations. In Atlantic City, infiltration of labor unions integral to the functioning of hotels and casinos (security guards, restaurant workers, bartenders) has allowed Cosa Nostra elements to extort and siphon gambling revenue. Illegal lotteries/numbers and sports betting are also multibillion dollar operations. In conjunction with its bookmaking interests, Cosa Nostra has a long history of infiltrating and corrupting professional and amateur athletics, including point-shaving scams and the virtual ownership of some professional boxers.[9]

Like gambling, the sex trade continues to flourish in the United States. In 1976, federal officials estimated the dollar volume of the pornography industry at $4 billion annually.[10] Significant mark-ups on sexually explicit movies and books generate huge profits. Cosa Nostra families operate pornography rings that are national in scope and vertically integrated, controlling, in many cases, production, distribution, and retailing. Competitive advantages in the porn industry are typically engineered through strong-arm tactics and include requiring producers to process film at organized crime-owned labs, forcing producers to distribute through organized crime-controlled companies under threat of piracy, burglarizing independent retail outlets, and intimidating theater owners into screening pirated versions of organized crime-controlled films. In Los Angeles, officials believe that 80 percent of the production and distribution of pornographic materials is controlled by Cosa Nostra and other organized criminals.[11]

Cosa Nostra's control of air, rail, and water freight terminals (through union infiltrations and employer associations) has provided crooks with billions of dollars in easily plundered cargo. The extent of theft, fraud, and extortion is far ranging and has reached into the realm of so-called "white-collar" crime. A 1997 *Business Week* article reported that organized crime groups had infiltrated Wall Street, running up stock prices, cashing out early, and extorting money from Wall Street brokers and traders. Cosa Nostra thugs have physically assaulted brokers and traders to "persuade" them to stay away from certain stocks and to artificially inflate others. Through the use of front men, it is estimated that Cosa Nostra families control as many as two dozen brokerage firms and influence many others.[12] In June 2000, federal law enforcers announced the indictment of 120 individuals, including members of all five New York City Cosa Nostra families and the Bor Russian organized crime group, for manipulating penny stocks and strong-arming brokers. The suspects were accused of conspiring to use bribery, extortion, and even soliciting murder to further frauds that reaped in excess of $50 million.[13] Another good example of merging organized and white-collar crime activities is the infamous savings and loan (S&L) crisis of the 1980s and 1990s. At least twenty-two failed S&Ls have been linked to joint money-laundering ventures by the CIA and organized crime figures. In fact, the spoils from plundered savings and loan institutions were even the subject of "sit-downs" between some of New York City's Cosa Nostra families.[14]

Although Robert Kennedy's Justice Department did undertake a serious federal crusade against the Italian syndicates in the early 1960s, the first sustained attack on Cosa Nostra began in the latter part of that decade with the passage of appropriate legislation. Title III of the Omnibus Crime Control and Safe Streets Act of 1968 provided for judicially approved electronic surveillance by federal, state, and local law enforcement officials. Amendments in 1986 authorized roving surveillance, thus enhancing the government's legal authority to monitor criminal activities. Not surprisingly, intercepted conversations have been a component of nearly every major Cosa Nostra prosecution over the last thirty years. The Racketeer Influenced and Corrupt Organizations statute (RICO) has been an especially useful tool, making it a crime to participate in or conduct the affairs of an enterprise through a "pattern of racketeering activity." RICO removed the constraints on prosecutors, allowing them to try in a single case multiple criminal defendants as a group—in short, law enforcement was no longer attacking distinct criminal acts, but entire *patterns* of criminal activity.[15] Although there exists no precise figure on how many criminal and civil cases were brought against organized crime in the 1980s, FBI Director William Sessions testified before a Senate subcommittee that, between 1981 and 1988, nineteen bosses, thirteen underbosses, and forty-three capos (crew chiefs/captains) had been convicted. At the same hearing, the director of the GAO's Office of Special Investigations stated that, between 1983 and 1986, there had been 2,500 indictments of Cosa Nostra figures. One of the more significant cases was *U.S. v. Salerno*, in which four of the five New York City bosses were convicted. The federal UNIRAC investigation of the International Longshoremen's Association led to the conviction of 130 businessmen, union officials, and Cosa Nostra figures. Other significant efforts against organized crime during this period were the civil RICO suits filed against Local 560 (controlled by the Genovese family since the 1950s) and against the International Brotherhood of Teamsters, its executive board, and the board's incumbents. Various consent decrees in those cases have had some success in purging Cosa Nostra figures from the Teamsters.[16] The case *U.S. v. Badalamenti*, commonly referred to as the "Pizza Connection" case, highlighted the transnational dimensions of Cosa Nostra. In that episode, a cooperative effort among American, Italian, Swiss, Brazilian, and Spanish law enforcement agencies broke up a network of American Cosa Nostra and Sicilian Mafia groups who had been using state-side pizzerias as fronts for their $1.6 billion heroin and money laundering enterprise.[17] The most famous New York crime buster of this era was Rudolph Giuliani, who gained national fame when he secured the conviction of crime boss Carmine Persico and eight other members of the Colombo crime family for racketeering in the New York City construction industry. Giuliani subsequently became mayor of New York City in 1993 and is credited with lowering the city's crime rate throughout the 1990s and bringing about reforms in the construction industry, the Fulton Fish Market, and waste hauling. In the 1990s, Manhattan District Attorney Robert Morgantheau engineered important prosecutions against racketeers at the Javits Center and in the garment and waste-hauling industries. Notorious gangsters convicted of crimes in the 1990s included Gambino crime boss John Gotti in 1992, Genovese boss Vincent "the Chin" Gigante in 1997, and John Gotti Jr. in 1999.[18]

Unfortunately, this massive law enforcement effort has not precipitated the demise of the Italian-American Cosa Nostra. In recent decades, organized criminals have been prominently involved in fuel-related tax scams, costing New York State billions in lost excise tax revenue. A cabal of criminals have perpetrated these crimes and have included organized criminals newly migrated to the United States (especially from Eastern Europe and Russia), energy industry executives in the United States and Europe, a variety of individuals and institutions involved in a vast money laundering operation, and Cosa Nostra members primarily from the New York Metropolitan region. Lawrence Iorizzo, a convicted tax evader who testified at a

House Ways and Means hearing, explained one of the common rackets: Conspirators incorporated numerous firms leaving a paper trail showing tax-free gasoline sales from one company to another until the final company responsible for paying the tax would simply vanish. One such New York–based operation reached to New Jersey, Connecticut, and Florida and stole about $8 million *per week* in gas taxes.[19]

Of course, even if the Italian syndicates have been weakened, the reality is that Cosa Nostra is but one small part of transnational and organized crime in the United States. The 1980s and 1990s have been characterized by the increasing prominence of numerous transnational crime groups operating in the United States, including African American, Latino, Chinese, Jamaican, Korean, Vietnamese, Japanese, Nigerian, Colombian, and Russian networks. If Cosa Nostra is in decline, then it seems obvious that other groups are filling the void. Prison gangs and outlaw motorcycle gangs have also coordinated large-scale criminal enterprises nationwide. The Hell's Angels, Pagans, Warlocks, and Outlaws have been especially active in the distribution of illicit drugs (especially methamphetamines), the porn industry, and contract killings.[20] Obviously, the law enforcement attack against Cosa Nostra, while impressive, has been directed at only one tentacle of what has been appropriately described as an octopus.

OUTLAW MOTORCYCLE GANGS

Outlaw motorcycle gangs are a continuing organized crime threat. The number of gangs operating in the United States is unknown; however, the U.S. Marshal's Service has estimated their number at 800 nationwide, while the Pennsylvania Crime Commission has suggested that the number is more like 200 to 400. Most gangs are small, local, and unorganized, but a few have evolved into large criminal organizations that are national and even international in scope. Outlaw motorcycle gangs participate in a wide variety of criminal activities, including murder for hire, prostitution, the operation of "massage parlors," international white slavery, kidnapping, burglary, gunrunning, insurance frauds, loan sharking, motorcycle and automobile theft, gambling, truck hijacking, arson, forgery of government documents, extortion, the fencing of stolen goods, theft from U.S. military bases, assault, rape, and, most notably, narcotics trafficking (especially methamphetamines, cocaine, and steroids).[21] In 1986, the President's Commission on Organized Crime estimated that outlaw motorcycle gangs controlled 40 percent of the entire U.S. methamphetamine supply. Other sources have estimated that the larger, well-organized groups earn up to $1 billion a year from their various criminal endeavors. The largest and most sophisticated groups operating today are the Hell's Angels, the Outlaws, the Pagans, and the Bandidos. All but the Pagans have international memberships, while the FBI has estimated that the Hell's Angels have more than sixty "chapters" in thirteen countries. Other noteworthy clubs operating in the United States include the Avengers (located primarily in Michigan, Ohio, and West Virginia), the Gypsy Jokers (Pacific Northwest), the Hessians (Las Vegas, Nevada), the Dirty Dozen (Arizona), the Vargos (California), the Sons of Silence (Colorado), and the Warlocks (southeastern Pennsylvania, Delaware, and New Jersey).[22]

Motorcycle gangs first appeared in the western United States following World War II when some veterans returning from war found it difficult to adjust to civilian life. These men gravitated to one another and formed loose-knit clubs that soon gained the reputation for fast riding, hard drinking, and toughness. In particular, their motorcycles became a symbol of their rebelliousness and outlaw spirit. National attention first focused on gang members in 1946 when several biker groups raided the town of Hollister, California. The incident made national headlines and inspired the annual July Fourth "run"—an important outlaw motorcycle gang tradition. The Hollister raid is also credited with inspiring the 1954 film *The Wild Ones*, a Hollywood production starring Marlon Brando, that glorified the outlaw biker subculture and aided the gangs in recruitment. Still, even the largest of the gangs were virtually unknown outside of California until the late 1960s. Ironically, law enforcement provided the impetus for renewed interest in motorcycle gangs when in 1965 the attorney general of California published the violent activities of the Hell's Angels in his annual report. This precipitated media coverage in the *New York Times*, *Time*, and *Newsweek*, and two years later, another Hollywood film, *Hell's Angels on Wheels*, once again boosted motorcycle clubs into the spotlight. Just as veterans returning from World War II supplied club members in the late 1940s, veterans from the Vietnam War were recruited in the late 1960s and early 1970s. At about the same time, biker gangs cashed in on the "hippie drug culture" by supplying narcotics to the growing number of U.S. consumers. By the early 1970s, several outlaw biker gangs had emerged as "highly-structured" and "somewhat disciplined" criminal organizations.[23]

One of the most striking features of outlaw motorcycle gangs is their highly formal, hierarchical authority structure, complete with specialized units and written bylaws. Members pay weekly dues, and local chapters pass on a percentage to the national headquarters of the given club. The largest gangs have a "mother club" with thirteen to twenty members, each of whom has authority over chapters in different regions. The mother club serves as national headquarters and is the final policy and rule-making body. The president of the mother club is the national president—he has authority over all members in all chapters. The vice president of the mother club takes over if the president cannot serve. Next in line of authority are territorial or regional representatives who handle problems that local chapters are unable to resolve. The national secretary-treasurer handles the club's money and is responsible for collecting dues from local chapters. The secretary-treasurer also records minutes of club meetings and drafts new club bylaws. Typically, there is also a position at the national level for an "enforcer," a powerful member who sees that the president's orders are carried out. In each local chapter, there are positions for president, vice president, secretary-treasurer, sergeant at arms, and road captain. The sergeant at arms is essentially the local equivalent of "enforcer," while road captains act as logisticians and security for club "runs" or outings.[24]

Although officers are elected for fixed terms, "informal leaders" often emerge who have as much or more power than the officers. The formal structure of the club may be separate from its "economic structure," which tends to be decentralized. For example, income-generating activities such as narcotics trafficking often involve operationally independent units composed of member and nonmember associates who work together in small groups. Each member of a motorcycle gang may have from four to ten nonmember associates, who in turn have their own network of accomplices. In essence, each club member is the hub of a criminal network that operates independently or in a partnership arrangement. Nonmember associates are often used as insulation to "buffer" club members from actual criminal involvement. Associates who market drugs and other illicit goods and services are required to pass a percentage along to the local chapter and the mother chapter (the mother chapter typically receives 10 percent of all profits).[25]

Outlaw motorcycle gangs often compete with one another in the distribution of narcotics and territory, but they have also been know to cooperate and even coordinate their illegal enterprises with other organized crime groups, including Cosa Nostra. For example, the New York chapter of the Hell's Angels has been linked to the operation of a Gambino crime family nightclub. Cleveland's more "traditional" organized crime groups have been known to use Hell's Angels members as enforcers and hit men. Other clubs have cooperated with Colombian and Cosa Nostra drug wholesalers. Likewise, leaders of the Pagans have been linked to the Cosa Nostra families in Pittsburgh and Philadelphia.[26]

A penchant for violent behavior is the trademark of outlaw motorcycle gangs and the source of the fear they generate. No crime or behavior can be too outrageous for club members. In addition, gangs have become more dangerous in recent years as the sophistication of their weaponry has increased. Police raids have resulted in the seizure of antitank weapons, plastic explosives, remote control detonators, and bulletproof vests. Although much of the violence is random and impulsive, other violence is instrumental and functional, aimed at protecting drug territories, intimidating witnesses, and facilitating extortion or contract murders. Violence among different clubs is not uncommon, but numerous examples of intergang cooperation exist in the provision of illegal goods and services, and inside of prisons for protection.[27]

Formerly the "Pissed Off Bastards of Bloomington," the Hell's Angels are the largest and most notorious of the outlaw motorcycle clubs. The organization has chapters in thirteen countries including the United States. Other major motorcycle gangs have essentially copied the Hell's Angels in organizational structure and operating style. In addition to the raid on the town of Hollister, California, which brought national attention to motorcycle gangs for the first time, the Angels are best known for the security stint at the Rolling Stones "Gimme Shelter" concert in Oakland in 1969. One club member stabbed and killed a concertgoer, but was acquitted at trial. A Justice Department trial of Ralph "Sonny" Barger (the national president) lasted for eight months during 1979 and 1980—the result was a hung jury. Incidents like these gave the group cause to boast that they were above the law. Today, with chapters in the United States, Canada, England, Switzerland, New Zealand, and Australia, the Hell's Angels have many aging members. It has been reported that chapter presidents, bloated with illicit wealth, have given up their cut-off jackets and Harleys for three-piece suits and Mercedes. Some clubhouses in New York and California are large buildings or complexes guarded with surveillance equipment and military weaponry. The club insignia is a winged skull.[28]

The Outlaws have some forty chapters with about 400 members in the United States, Canada, and Australia. The group originated in Chicago in the 1950s, but is now headquartered in Detroit. In the United States, members are found from Florida to New York and as far west as Oklahoma. The Outlaws are involved in a wide range of criminal activities, including contract murder, car theft, extortion, and drug trafficking (especially cocaine and valium). Members of the Outlaws killed three Hell's Angels in 1974—the feud between the two has been ongoing ever since. The club mascot is a skull over crossed pistons known as "Charlie," copied from Marlon Brando's jacket in the movie *The Wild Ones.*

The Pagans originated in Prince George County, Maryland, in 1959. The group has steadily increased its size since then by merging with smaller clubs. Law enforcement officials estimate that the Pagans have twenty-six chapters with some 500 members. Their increased size resulted in the founding of a mother club, consisting of the original thirteen members. Unlike other motorcycle gangs, the Pagans run chapters directly under the authority of the mother club. Recently, federal RICO prosecutions have imprisoned many Pagan leaders. The group's colors feature the Norse fire god. The Bandidos are the third largest and fastest growing motorcycle gang in the United States. The group has at least 300 members and twenty-two chapters, with international posts in Australia and Marseilles, France. The gang was established in 1966 and began trafficking heroin in 1975. Methampehtamine and cocaine distribution are favored today. The Bandidos are bureaucratically structured with four vice presidents, one of whom serves as president. Activities are centered in Texas, while the Frito Bandido is their mascot.[29]

THE YAKUZA

The Boryokudon, or Yakuza, can be traced back to the early 1600s, when renegade samarai roved the countryside terrorizing Japanese villages. As an organized group, the Yakuza began to flourish in the later 1700s, when groups of gamblers, street peddlers, and hoodlums banded together. The power of the Yakuza grew rapidly during the Allied occupation of Japan after World War II; by 1963, there were more than 184,000 Yakuza members organized into some 5,200 gangs. Intergang warfare has reduced their numbers somewhat. Estimates of Yakuza size vary from 60,000 to 110,000 members loosely organized into "families," each led by the *oyabun*, or father. Yakuza members boast extensive body tattooing, are required to be blindly obedient to the father, and are known to sever the top joint of the little finger as an act of fealty and/or contrition to the *oyabun*.

By the early 1980s, the most significant Yakuza faction, the Yamaguchi-gumi, controlled more than 2,500 legal and illegal businesses and was composed of over 500 street-level gangs that grossed $500 million annually. Gang warfare in the 1980s and the passing of an anti-Yakuza law by the Japanese government in 1992 has not diminished the Yakuza in any significant way, and the confederation of crime gangs continues to be involved in every aspect of the Japanese economy. Yakuza gangs own large amounts of real estate and sport and entertainment businesses, and are heavily involved in the distribution of amphetamines, the control of casinos and brothels, loan sharking, and extortion and protection rackets centering on Japanese corporations and banks. Yakuza enforcers forcibly evict tenants from their homes to make way for new construction projects and to keep corporate meetings "short and quiet." Japan's Finance Ministry believes that as much as $600 billion to $1 trillion in bad debts are owed to Japanese banks by Yakuza-affiliated real estate speculators—the bankers are afraid to liquidate or collect. One such banker who attempted to collect on a delinquent Yakuza loan in 1994 was executed in his home. The extent of the Yakuza's influence in Japan is exemplified by the fact that the "black economy" accounts for 4.5 percent of the national output. In 1999, tax evasion, drug trafficking, prostitution, gambling, and other gangster activities totaled $194 billion.[30]

The Yakuza is truly a transnational criminal organization, ranking only behind the Chinese Triads in size. Yakuza gangs are found in South Korea, Australia, Costa Rica, Brazil, Hawaii, and every major city on the West Coast of the United States. Yakuza gangs are heavily involved in the smuggling of amphetamines and firearms from the United States to Japan. (Strict gun controls in Japan transform a $100 American handgun into a product worth $1,200 in Japan.) The principal impact of the Yakuza on the United States is its purchase of legitimate businesses to launder and repatriate its illegally earned revenues. A Yakuza affiliate, the Rondan Doyukai Company, is believed to have purchased shares in the Dow Chemical Company, Chase Manhattan, IBM, General Motors, Bank of America, and Atlantic Richfield. Japanese gangs have acquired interests in or purchased import/export, real estate, restaurant, and oil lease businesses in Hawaii and Los Angeles, and have reportedly established themselves in cities like Denver, Las Vegas, and San Francisco.[31]

CHINESE TRIADS

The Triad is one of many secret Chinese societies formed originally as a resistance movement to the Ch'ing Dynasty that ruled China from the early seventeenth century to 1911. After the ruling Manchus were deposed in 1911, the Triad focused its activities on opiate trafficking. Today, there are five or six primary Triad groups with many smaller satellite groups that together form the world's largest criminal association with over 100,000 members. Triad groups are tightly structured and hierarchical, much like a corporation. The largest and most powerful group is the Sun Yee On, based in Hong Kong. The Sun Yee On has links with the Communist government in Beijing and is involved in extortion, heroin trafficking, and alien smuggling in Australia, Thailand, Canada, and Central America. In Taiwan, the United Bamboo gang has 15,000 members and has spread far beyond Taiwanese borders. The Triad groups with a presence in the United States are the Sun Yee On, 14K, Wo Hop To, Wo On Lok, and Leun Kung Lok. These groups are especially prevalent in the Pacific Rim, with a strong presence in Hawaii, Seattle, Vancouver, and San Francisco. Triads are also prevalent in the eastern cities of New York, Boston, and Toronto.[32]

Triads control the eastern Asian heroin trade, with annual profits over $200 billion. Other principal transnational criminal activities include the smuggling of weapons, cars, boats, electronic equipment, and people. The smuggling of illegal aliens into Europe and North America nets an additional $3.5 billion per year. In 1992, the U.S. leader of the Wo Hop To Triad was indicted for the illegal importation of AK-47 assault rifles, heroin trafficking, murder for hire, gambling, loan sharking, and money laundering.[33] In China, as the mainland opens up to the world, Triad members from Hong Kong, Taiwan, and overseas Chinatowns are swelling the ranks of the several thousand individual Triad societies in the country. In 2001, "mafia-style" crimes increased by 530 percent in China, while 2,600 influential Chinese officials were implicated in crimes that included corruption and collusion with Chinese organized criminals.[34] With a strong presence in the United States, the proliferation of the Triads in China suggests they are an increasing transnational threat.

GANGS FROM RUSSIA AND OTHER FORMER SOVIET REPUBLICS

Although organized crime in Russia dates back many centuries, the collapse of the Soviet Union precipitated the explosion of organized crime in the former Soviet Republics and its satellite states in Eastern Europe. The number of gangs thought to comprise the Russian "Mafiya" grew from 785 in 1990 to more than 8,000 by 1996. The more highly structured syndicates number closer to 300, of which the Brigade of the Sun, the Odessa Mafia, and Armenian Organized Crime Groups are dominant.

Although the numbers vary depending on the source, more than one hundred Russian organized crime gangs are thought to operate in forty-four countries around the world.[35]

In Russia, former Communist Party elites, KGB officers, and Mafiya gang members have plundered resources once controlled by the state. Capital flight from Russia is especially serious, with criminals laundering some $1.5 to $3 billion per month into offshore accounts. The Russian Institute for Banking and Financial Managers has estimated that 70 to 80 percent of private banks in Russia are owned or controlled by organized crime, while authorities believe that 40 percent of the Russian economy is linked to organized crime. The Ukrainian Economic and Political Research Center has concluded that the "shadow economy" in Ukraine had grown to 60 percent of the gross domestic product by 1996. The political leadership in those states directs organized crime in Russia, Georgia, Ukraine, and Kazakhstan. In fact, the Russian Mafiya counts as members much of the old ruling class, or "nomenklatura," and the KGB. Principal criminal activities include currency and arms smuggling, prostitution, racketeering, murder for hire, credit card theft, automobile theft, slavery and human smuggling, the smuggling of nuclear materials, the illegal export of raw materials (especially diamonds), and narcotics trafficking. Mafiya groups have established a heroin pipeline that stretches from Myanmar to the Balkans to German and Nigeria, and on to Europe and the United States.[36]

James R. Richards states that the Russian Mafiya is active in most large American cities. Since the mid-1970s, Brighton Beach, New York, has been the traditional base of Russian organized crime in America, but the FBI has identified Russian crime groups in Boston, Chicago, Miami, Cleveland, Philadelphia, Seattle, Denver, Minneapolis, Dallas, Los Angeles, San Francisco, and San Diego. Their proliferation has been considerable: In 1993, the FBI stated there were fifteen Mafiya groups operating in the United States. In 2001, researchers at the Justice Department's National Institute of Justice reported that there were some thirteen to fifteen loosely categorized crime groups with international ties to Russia or other former Soviet Republics operating in the United States, with a total membership in the country between 500 and 600. Russian crime groups in American are involved in a broad variety of crimes, including telecommunications fraud and the cloning of cellular phones, money laundering, and medical and insurance fraud— staged auto accidents and false billing schemes are favorites. In an infamous 1991 case involving two Russian émigrés, the criminals established mobile medical laboratories that conducted false tests on patients and sent inflated bills to insurance companies that netted the perpetrators $1 billion. In another case from 1992 to 1994, a Pittsburgh medical clinic owned by the Mafiya paid Russian émigrés to fake accidents and injuries and file false claims totaling $5 million.[37]

Fuel racketeering is a prominent Russian organized crime scam that results in the loss of $2 billion in U.S. federal and state gasoline taxes annually. In a typical "daisy-chain" operation, criminals falsify tax documents and incorporate shell companies (shells are corporations that exist only on paper) to avoid paying taxes. Companies in the chain pay the tax but receive a credit once the gas is distributed to the other companies down the line. By the time auditors determine what entity is ultimately responsible for paying the tax, the fictitious company and its owners are long gone. Other common gas tax frauds include extending fuel by adding tax-free additives, rigging fuel pumps, over-reporting fuel oil sales to government subsidized housing, mixing low-grade fuels with butane in order to increase the octane level, and manipulating dyed agricultural fuels (not taxed) and selling them as regular gasoline. One good example of Russian fuel racketeering involved members of the Mikaelian organization of the Armenian Mafiya, indicted in 1995 for using falsified wholesale permits to buy tax-free diesel fuel and re-selling to various independent Russian-operated gas stations.[38]

The Russian Mafiya in America is not limited in the extent of their criminal ventures. Russian gangs have targeted U.S. banks and financial institutions. In one recent case, the criminals perpetrated an investment fraud scheme and laundered $2 million in profits through the Bank of New York. In 1999, four individuals and two companies were charged with laundering between $7 billion and $10 billion in criminal proceeds and legitimate assets through institutions like the Bank of New York, helping organized criminals and otherwise legitimate Russian businesspeople to evade Russian tax authorities. Russian organized crime has been implicated in the white slave trade in Buffalo, Russian waste disposal businesses dump toxic wastes into tankers carrying gasoline to be burned in automobiles, and in 1997 two Russian criminals were caught trying to deliver tactical nuclear weapons and surface-to-air missiles to U.S. buyers. In another case, a task force investigating Russian organized crime in south Florida uncovered the intended sale of a Russian submarine to Colombian drug traffickers. Posing as a geological company looking to map the ocean floor, the criminals were nabbed while negotiating the purchase of the sub for later distribution to the Colombians.[39]

COLOMBIAN AND MEXICAN DRUG CARTELS

Some of the most significant transnational organized crime groups affecting the United States are the various drug trafficking organizations centered in the South American countries of Colombia and Mexico. The Colombian drug trade alone is thought to generate $5 billion annually, with some 300 Colombian trafficking organizations operating within the United States. In 1995, the DEA estimated that cocaine produced in South America (virtually all coca is grown in Peru, Bolivia, and Colombia) amounted to about 715 metric tons. Historically, most of this supply has been provided by the Medellin and Cali cocaine cartels. Established around 1978 and run by infamous traffickers like Fabio and Jorge Ochoa, Pablo Escobar, and Carlos Lehder, the Medellin cartel has now been decimated by the arrest and killing of key leaders. By the early 1990s, the Cali cartel had replaced the Medellin cartel as Colombia's primary cocaine trafficking organization. During the 1990s, the Cali organization produced and distributed 80 to 90 percent of the cocaine imported and consumed in the United States. Successful interdiction by U.S. authorities forced the Cali traffickers to shift their shipment routes from the Caribbean to Mexico, contracting with Mexican criminals to smuggle contraband across the southwest border of the United States. While the increasing prominence of the Mexican cartels—originally paid $1,000 to $2,000 per kilo, they now get paid between 40 and 50 percent of the cocaine product itself—has limited Cali profits, if the cartel were a legitimate corporation, it would rank first in gross profits of $8 billion per year, topping Exxon, General Electric, Philip Morris, and IBM. A joint U.S.-Colombian crackdown in 1995 and 1996 led to the arrest of seven of the eight leading Cali cartel kingpins, including Gilberto and Miguel Rodriguez-Orejuela, Jose Santacruz Londono, and Pacha Herrera Buitrago.[40]

Operations directed against the Peru-Colombian aerial supply route for cocaine base and additional arrests against remaining Medellin cartel members in the period 1995 to 1997 precipitated a transition in the South American drug trade. This included a shift in supply routes to Mexico, Venezuela, and the eastern Caribbean, a shift in production to other countries like Brazil, and the rise of independent trafficking groups in Peru, Bolivia, Mexico, Argentina, Chile, Paraguay, and Uruguay. Two new prominent Colombian trafficking organizations to emerge from the 1995–1997 offensives against Cali are the Cartel de la Costa and the Northern Valle del Cauca. These organizations operate in the Caribbean coastal area, including Cartagena, and model themselves after the old Medellin traffickers by running smaller, extremely violent groups as opposed to the rigidly structured businesslike enterprises of the Cali traffickers. These new Colombia cartels have shifted to Caribbean routes because Puerto Rican and Dominican distributors charge less for transport than the Mexican cartels. The Northern Valle del Cauca group also distributes to the United States a huge volume of heroin—about 50 percent of heroin consumed in the United States now comes from Colombia. The overall supply of cocaine to the United States, like demand, has not decreased.[41]

The shift in cocaine trafficking routes through Mexico in the late 1980s empowered Mexican crime groups and gave rise to the Mexican Federation, consisting of the Gulf, Juarez, Sonora, and Tijuana cartels. These Mexican cartels control almost all of the heroin, cocaine, and marijuana production, smuggling, and distribution in Mexico and the western United States. A fifth group, the Amezqua organization, controls the burgeoning methamphetamine trade. The cartels of the Mexican Federation launder the equivalent of 2.5 percent of Mexico's economic value, or about $7 billion annually. Until his death from liposuction complications in 1997, Amado Carrillo-Fuentes was the leader of the Juarez cartel, considered the most significant in the Mexican Federation. Carillo-Fuentes had been aligned with the Rodriguez-Orejuela family and elements of the Medellin cartel, and was known as "Lord of the Skies" for pioneering trafficking using large aircraft. Since his death, there has been a murderous struggle within the Juarez organization and from the Arellano-Felix organization (the Tijuana cartel) for control. Notwithstanding the violent competition, the Juarez cartel now controls the New York cocaine market once dominated by the Cali cartel. As with the Colombian traffickers, Mexican cartel leaders have been arrested and incarcerated in recent years. Juan Garcia Abrego of the Gulf cartel was arrested in 1996, and Sonora cartel head Miguel Caro-Quintero has been incarcerated since 1989. Nevertheless, Caro-Quintero still runs the Sonora cartel from his Mexican prison cell, while the Gulf cartel remains operational. The Tijuana cartel, run by Alberto Benjamin Arellano-Felix and his six brothers and four sisters, is the most violent of the Mexican drug trafficking organizations. Ramon Eduardo Arellano-Felix operated a San-Diego "security firm" called the Logan Heights Calle 30, responsible for multiple homicides in southern California, as well as the 1993 slaying of a Roman Catholic cardinal at the Guadalajara airport. The Tijuana cartel is believed to pay $1 million a week in bribes to Mexican judges, prosecutors, police, army, and customs officials.[42] In March 2002, the DEA announced the arrest of Benjamin Arellano-Felix and confirmed the death of his brother Ramon in a shootout.[43]

Events that are more recent suggest that the structure of the Mexican drug trade may be changing from broad oversight by a few powerful cartels to a market inhabited by smaller more businesslike gangs that fight less among themselves but react violently to police pressure. Law enforcement pressure against the cartels has been intense: In March 2003, Mexican Defense Secretary General Gerardo Vega Garcia announced the capture of Osiel Cardenas, the head of the Gulf cartel. Cardenas was believed to lead an army of 300 hit men and drug traffickers in the Gulf coast state of Tamaulipas and was so powerful that he enlisted dozens of Mexican police as bodyguards. While the arrest was unlikely to dismantle the cartel, General Vega Garcia contends that the cartels have been fragmented, a condition that actually makes it more difficult to identify new leaders.[44]

ITALIAN-BASED TRANSNATIONAL CRIME GROUPS

The Sicilian Mafia is the most powerful of the Italian-based transnational crime groups and has supplied the structural model adopted by Italian-American/La Cosa Nostra crime groups in the United States. The Sicilian Mafia is certainly one of the most prolific of all the transnational crime organizations, operating in more than forty countries including the United

States. The FBI concluded that the infiltration of the Sicilian Mafia into the United States occurred primarily from the late 1970s onward, with about 3,000 members operating primarily in Northeastern and Mid-Atlantic states by the early 1990s. Consisting of approximately 180 "families" or clans, the Sicilian Mafia has accumulated most of its political and economic power from the vast profits generated through trafficking in heroin. After law enforcers broke up the infamous "French Connection" in 1972, forcing French Corsicans who controlled the U.S. heroin market out of business, the Sicilian Mafia stepped in to fill the void; by 1981, the group was smuggling six tons into the United States annually. There have been some significant law enforcement successes against the group in Italy and the United States. In September 1997, thirty-one high-ranking Sicilian Mafia members were convicted of murder in the 1992 assassination of Giovanni Falcone, once Italy's top organized crime prosecutor. Also convicted was Salvatore "Toto" Riina, the Mafia's reputed "boss of bosses." Today the group is thought to be responsible for $750 million worth of Southeast Asian heroin entering New York City each year and, along with the South American cartels, remains one of the principal heroin suppliers to U.S. consumers. France's Foreign Intelligence Service has estimated that $20 billion per year in laundered crime profits are repatriated to Palermo, Italy, the traditional base of the crime group.[45]

Another major Italian transnational crime gang is the Camorra, begun in the 1820s by inmates in Neapolitan prisons. The power of the gangs quickly grew until their influence spread beyond the prisons into the city of Naples, and by 1830 elements of the working class in Campania perceived the Camorra as equal in power to a branch of the Italian government. Recent estimates suggest that the Camorra comprises about thirty clans with 6,000 members. Its principal criminal activities are extortion, drug trafficking, and cigarette smuggling. Many Camorra members and associates fled Italian justice and gang warfare and immigrated to the United States in the 1980s. By 1993, the FBI believed there were 200 Camorra members in the country. Although there appears to be no clan structure in the United States, Camorra members have established a criminal presence in Cleveland, Los Angeles, Albany, and Springfield, Massachusetts. U.S. law enforcement considers the Camorra a rising criminal enterprise, especially dangerous because of its willingness to ally itself with other criminal organizations. In 1995, the Camorra and the Russian Mafiya cooperated in a scheme in which the Camorra would bleach out U.S. $1.00 bills and reprint them as $100s, then transport them to the Mafiya for distribution in twenty-nine Eastern Bloc and former Soviet Republics. The Russian criminals paid the Camorra with property and firearms. The Camorra was hit hard in 1997 when Italian police seized $285 million in assets, including buildings, land holdings, companies, race horses, automobiles, and stocks and bonds.[46]

The 'Ndrangheta, also called the "Honored Society," may have formed in the 1860s when a group of Sicilians was cast out of Sicily and settled in the Italian province of Calabria. They soon formed small criminal societies that evolved into a political power with the support of Calabrian peasants. With about 5,300 members at present, the 'Ndrangheta is very active in the heroin trade. A U.S. investigation that ended in 1989 found that the group had used pizza shops in East Coast cities to sell their heroin and a New York travel agency to launder the profits. A more recent 1997 effort, code-named Operation Cat's Eye, discovered a heroin trafficking enterprise run by the 'Ndrangheta from Toronto, Canada, and Tampa, Florida. As of 1993, there were perhaps 200 'Ndrangheta members in the United States, with criminal activities documented in Los Angeles, Miami, Tampa, Baltimore, and Wilmington. The FBI believes that 'Ndrangheta activities in the United States may be controlled by cells in Italy and Canada.[47]

OTHER TRANSNATIONAL GROUPS OPERATING IN THE UNITED STATES

African criminal enterprises impacting the United States are predominantly Nigerian in origin; however, the FBI notes that some criminal groups are based in other nations such as Liberia and Ghana. The FBI has identified a transnational African organized crime presence in cities from coast to coast, but conclude that they are most prevalent in Atlanta, Baltimore, Washington, D.C., Chicago, Milwaukee, Dallas, Houston, New York, and Newark. The U.S. State Department estimates that Nigerian criminal gangs working as subcontractors for the Russian Mafiya, Chinese Triads, Colombian cartels, or the various Italian criminal groups import as much as 40 percent of the heroin smuggled into the United States. Since the mid-1980s, over one thousand Nigerian nationals have been convicted of smuggling heroin into the United States. In 1994, Interpol found that Nigerians were the third largest ethnic drug smuggling groups in the world, and in 1998, the International Narcotics Control Strategy Report described Nigeria as the "hub of African narcotics traffic." Typically, Nigerian gangs use U.S. dollars to buy heroin from source countries such as Myanmar, Pakistan, and Afghanistan. Both drugs and firearms are smuggled over land and through ports to South Africa, and on to New York City and various European cities. Sales revenue is used to buy luxury products such as cars, electronics, and watches that are shipped to Nigeria for resale in the lucrative black market. Nigerian organized criminals are also known to be involved in cocaine trafficking, credit card scams, bank fraud, insurance fraud, ivory smuggling, the manufacture and use of false identifications, and advance-fee frauds (people are persuaded to advance money for the promise of incredible investment returns, which of course never materialize). A common fraud, called "419" scheme, after the section of the Nigerian penal code implicated, involves a deluge of letters, e-mails, and faxes proposing fictitious business opportunities in exchange for an advance fee. Scams like these are estimated to cost Americans some $250 million every year. Nigerian criminal organizations are believed to be active in some eighty countries around the world, and a survey of international business executives in 1996 ranked Nigeria's government as the most corrupt in the world.[48]

Beginning in the mid-1980s, gangs of Jamaican nationals, commonly called "posses," established a presence in the United States. Recent estimates place the number of Jamaican posses in the United States at about forty, with gang activity present in at least eighteen different American cities. United States–based membership is thought to be a staggering 100,000 individuals, most of whom are felons or illegal aliens. The Jamaicans are vertically integrated in the United States as importers, wholesalers, local distributors, and retailers of illicit drugs, particularly cocaine and marijuana. The posses have a reputation for being especially violent, and some groups such as the Dog, Jungle, and Okra Slime are even trained in guerilla warfare—800 drug-related murders were attributed to Jamaican gangs just in the period between 1984 and 1987. The Shower posse is considered to be the largest and most powerful of the Jamaican organized crime gangs, with a strong presence in both Miami and New York City. Posses are also known to be prominently involved in money laundering and in the smuggling of illegal firearms, such as mini-TEC 9s, Glock pistols, and AR-15 assault rifles.[49]

Canada

In 1998, the Department of the Solicitor General of Canada commissioned a study into the impact of organized crime on Canadian society. The office of the Solicitor General concluded that organized crime is a "national and international problem that undermines the social fabric of Canada and the health and safety of our communities." The Organized Crime Impact Study found that:

- the most reliable Canadian government estimate of the Canadian illicit drug market is between $7 billion to $10 billion each year;
- economic crime, such as securities fraud and telemarketing scams, costs Canadians at least $5 billion each year;

- between $5 and $17 billion is laundered in Canada each year;
- up to 16,000 people may be smuggled into Canada each year;
- the production and sale of counterfeit products—such as clothing, software, and pharmaceuticals—may cost Canadians over $1 billion each year;
- illegal smuggling of tobacco, alcohol, and jewelry may result in the loss of up to $1.5 billion in government tax revenues.[50]

In 1994 alone, Canadian chartered banks lost $143 million through fraud, while the insurance industry is thought to lose between $1.5 and $2 billion annually.[51] Government authorities and researchers agree that the last decades of the twentieth century witnessed the proliferation and increasing sophistication of organized criminal activities in Canada.[52]

In some ways, the development of organized crime in Canada mirrored its evolution in the United States. In the early twentieth century, the infamous "Black Hand" extorted money from Canadian businesses, and Prohibition in the United States facilitated an unprecedented expansion of organized crime in Canada (including the infiltration of legitimate industries like transportation and distilling). By the 1950s, Canadian organized crime groups had become widely involved in commercial and government fraud in the public and private sectors. More recently, police investigations have uncovered large-scale tax and insurance fraud and the counterfeiting of currency, credit cards, clothing, and computer software. The more sophisticated criminal groups corrupt industry officials and place operatives within legitimate firms to facilitate the laundering of their illicit wealth.[53]

Although the numbers of industries in Canada infiltrated by organized crime are myriad, the securities market is one sector of the economy that has been especially susceptible. During the 1950s, "Hamilton's Papalia family" extorted money and inside information from securities brokers, and from the 1950s to the early 1970s, Italian crime groups in Canada stole millions of dollars in securities certificates. A loan shark and money launderer for Montreal's once powerful Cotroni family was charged with fraudulently manipulating stock market shares over a fifteen-year period. More recently in the 1990s, Canadian police investigated the role of outlaw motorcycle gangs in manipulating the price of BioChem stock and exploding four bombs at the company's Laval headquarters. The corrosive effects of organized crime on private-sector industries and the Canadian securities market have been well documented and include corruption, violence, theft, and loss of market integrity.[54]

Organized crime groups have infiltrated and use Canada's marine ports as conduits for all manner of contraband, including drugs, tobacco, alcohol, firearms, gems, jewelry, cigars, animal parts, and even illegal migrants. Cross-border smugglers as well as domestic criminals supply the illicit tobacco and alcohol market in Canada (although recent changes in the tax structure may remove the attractiveness of moving tobacco products from lower tax to higher tax provinces).[55] Drug trafficking remains a primary source of illicit revenue for Canadian criminals and involves Asians, Italians, outlaw motor-cycle gangs, and, to a lesser extent Iranians, Romanians, Lebanese, and Jamaicans. Colombian-based cocaine trafficking groups are well established in Canada, while cooperation between groups is common. By the late 1990s, the hydroponic cultivation of marijuana had reached unprecedented levels—just one warehouse in Montreal housed a single hyrdoponic facility with 11,000 plants in full bloom. Much of this high-yielding THC-content mari-juana is exported from British Columbia to the United States. Outlaw motor-cycle gangs are the principal actors in a thriving illicit chemical trade (mostly PCP, methamphetamine, and LSD), while Asian syndicates with ties to Hong Kong, Taiwan, China, and Vietnam control the heroin market.[56]

Advances in technology have been exploited by sophisticated criminal organizations that use technology-based countersurveillance measures. Canadian criminal groups are using the Internet to communicate and con-ceal information, to manipulate the stock market, to sell illicit drugs, and to conduct illegal gambling. Credit card fraud, advance fee scams, and iden-tity theft are devastating to consumers and e-commerce sites—dollar losses from credit card rip-offs totaled $226.7 million in 1999. Major crime groups use the Internet to launder funds by bouncing them from account to account around the world.[57]

Lone criminals as well as criminal syndicates use computers and the Internet to prey upon children. The Central Intelligence Service Canada (CISC) observed in its 2001 Annual Report that the sexual exploitation of children is a continuing organized crime threat to Canadians. Pedophiles use computer networks to produce and distribute pornographic images and lure child victims. Canadian law enforcement agencies are receiving ever-increasing requests for assistance related to child pornography on the Internet. Two of the top ten global commercial Internet pornography sites emanate from Vancouver. Child prostitution is also a nationwide problem, but is most frequently reported in the larger urban centers of Western Canada. These growing threats and the belief by authorities that organized crime groups are involved precipitated a spate of national and provincial leg-islation in 2000 and 2001 aimed at combating the problem.[58]

Asian Organized Crime Groups

The CISC has noted that Asian-based organized crime (AOC) groups are extensively involved in a broad range of organized crime activities. These include cocaine trafficking; the production, traffic, and exportation of marijuana; the importation and distribution of heroin from Southeast Asia; the smuggling of illegal immigrants; theft (especially luxury automobiles, computers, computer components, and other electronic goods); prostitution; gambling; home invasions; shoplifting rings; kidnapping; extortion; the smuggling of cigarettes and liquor; insurance fraud; commodity smuggling; contract murders; and the production and distribution of counterfeit currency, software, pirated videos, manufactured goods, credit cards (most counterfeit credit card fraud in Canada is attributable to Asian criminal gangs), and debit cards. Like most significant organized crime groups, AOC groups launder their profits and invest criminal proceeds in legitimate businesses.[59] Based in the urban centers of Vancouver, Calgary, Edmonton, Toronto, and Montreal, AOC gangs are nevertheless increasingly expanding their operations to smaller cities and even rural areas. Moreover, Asian syndicates in Canada continue to promote their association with other organized crime groups at the regional, national, and international levels. Another hallmark of AOC activity in Canada is its mobility: Groups from Toronto and Montreal have used New Brunswick to distribute counterfeit currency, and Vietnamese gang members from Montreal were apprehended in St. John distributing counterfeit money produced by the Dai Huen Jai group in Toronto. Membership is fluid (members often operate several criminal enterprises simultaneously with members of allied AOC groups) and includes juvenile members of Asia street gangs. In fact, much of the observed increase in violence associated with Asian-based criminal activity can be attributed to Vietnamese, Laotian, and Cambodian street gangs.[60]

In addition to Asian street gangs, prominent AOC groups in Canada include several Chinese Triads (the Luen Kung Lok and 14K have had a historical presence in the country) and Dai Huen Jai, or the Big Circle Boys, centered in Toronto and British Columbia with ties to Hong Kong. The Lotus Gang, composed of Canadian-born Chinese, operates in Vancouver, has ties to the Hell's Angels, and is involved in cocaine and heroin trafficking, credit card fraud, extortion, and the cloning of cellular telephones. Fukienese crime groups are emerging in Toronto (the Fukienese dominate Asian organized crime in nearby New York City) and are prominently involved in the smuggling of migrants from Fuchow in China into Canada and the United States. In Quebec, over 350 Asian-based criminals are divided into thirty-five loosely structured gangs, most of which are national or international in scope. AOC activity in Montreal is dominated by Vietnamese or ethnic Chinese born in Vietnam.[61]

The importation and distribution of heroin and the smuggling of illegal migrants are two of the more noteworthy AOC activities. Asian-based organized crime groups are in fact the primary suppliers of Southeast Asian heroin imported into Canada, exercising near exclusive control over that trade. In September 2000, fifty-seven kilograms of heroin, seventeen kilograms of designer drug pills, and $1.2 million in cash were intercepted by law enforcement. The heroin was shipped by rail after arriving in Vancouver from Guangdong Province and was hidden in 1,700 plastic eggs among 174,000 real duck eggs. The smuggling of illegal migrants also continues to be a serious problem. In 1998, Canadian and U.S. authorities dismantled a smuggling ring that had moved as many as 3,600 Chinese from Fujian into New York State through Vancouver and Toronto. In April 2001, thirty-six illegal Chinese migrants were found in cargo ship containers in Vancouver destined for Long Beach, California. Earlier in the same month, twenty-three Chinese migrants were discovered in shipping containers in Long Beach. The migrants told officials that they paid AOC gangs between $45,000 and $55,000 for their voyage. The deportations of 599 Chinese migrants who were discovered in four ships off the coast of British Columbia in 1999 continued into 2001, and in February 2001, three men were convicted of attempting to smuggle 187 illegal Chinese migrants into Vancouver. The Akwesasne Mohawk Territory near Cornwall and the Walpole Island and Niagara areas are also major immigrant smuggling routes. In 1999 alone, 7,000 altered and counterfeit travel documents with a street value of $122 million were seized from AOC and other crime groups involved in migrant smuggling.[62]

In its 2001 annual report, the CISC provided an outlook for AOC groups. The CISC predicts the continuing dominance of Asian gangs in the smuggling of Chinese migrants, the importing of heroin from Southeast Asia, and an expansion of marijuana growing operations for export to the United States.[63]

Eastern European–Based Organized Crime (EEOC)

Eastern European–based organized crime groups made their first appearance in Toronto in the mid-1990s. Since that time, Canada has experienced a proliferation of criminal gangs originating from the former Soviet Union and the former communist states in Eastern Europe. Russian gangs are especially prevalent and operate in every part of the country. The CISC found that EEOC groups in Canada are part of a larger transnational Eastern

European criminal community and are well connected to counterparts in Russia, Europe, and the United States. The EEOC groups have forged alliances with other major organized crime groups in Canada; are most active in Toronto, Montreal, and Vancouver; but also maintain a considerable presence in Calgary, Edmonton, and Halifax. Toronto in particular seems to be an integral center for criminal gangs from the former Soviet Union.

EEOC gangs are indiscriminate in their choice of illicit activities, but are most prominently involved in prostitution, tobacco and weapons smuggling, immigration fraud, the importation of illegal drugs, the theft of vehicles for export (Russia is a major destination for stolen Canadian cars, which can be sold for twice their Canadian value), gas tax frauds, and money laundering. Financial frauds are common and include Internet scams such as credit card "skimming," e-commerce site hacking, and fraudulent credit card purchases. The establishment of shell companies and money laundering in order to move capital out of Eastern Europe increased significantly in 1998. Canadian and American businesses working with Russian companies soon discovered that the Russians did not possess the reported capital or else were involved in fronting money laundering ventures. Import and export companies and the West Coast fishing industry were most affected by these activities. The CISC has observed that the EEOC groups are becoming increasingly sophisticated, exploiting technology to perpetrate credit card and debit card schemes, using legitimate businesses to conceal and launder illicit income, and expanding their involvement in the drug trade and the smuggling of consumer commodities.

The presence of Russian-based organized crime in Canada has already produced significant damage in the country's financial sector. YBM Magnex International Incorporation, a Canadian industrial magnet manufacturer, collapsed in 1998 after allegations surfaced that the company was involved in laundering profits for the Russian mob. In May 2001, the Ontario Securities Commission held judicial hearings that included charges of securities law violations against ten former directors of YBM Magnex, the company's outside legal counsel, and two prominent brokerage houses. The Ontario Securities Commission alleges that YBM withheld knowledge of EEOC associations, thereby misleading potential investors in a 1997 prospectus prepared for a $100 million share issue.[64]

Italian-Based Organized Crime (IOC)

Italian organized criminals in Canada are associated with or belong to one of three main organizations: the Sicilian Mafia, the 'Ndrangheta, or the American Cosa Nostra. The Sicilian Mafia is considered the most powerful of the three and maintains ties to other Sicilian clans in Canada, the United States, Venezuela, and Italy. The main Sicilian organization is the Caruana/Cuntrera family. The three major Italian-based organized crime groups participate in joint ventures with all the major criminal entities in Canada, including Asian and Eastern European–based gangs, outlaw motorcycle gangs, South American groups, and domestic criminal organizations. The Italians most notably associate with the other gangs in the importation of drugs and the provision of money laundering services.

Italian-based crime members are prominently involved in drug trafficking, illegal gaming (sport betting, video lottery terminals, backroom casinos), money laundering, extortion, and loan-sharking. In Western Canada, IOC groups are heavily invested in legitimate businesses such as construction, food supplies and services, and restaurants and coffee bars. The influence of IOC groups extends into businesses as diverse as real estate, construction, hotels, paving and asphalt, and automobiles. Italian organized criminals in Canada who provided protection for hundreds of Russian-owned gas stations, permitting the existence of a "cartel" for supply and distribution, facilitated racketeering in gasoline and U.S.-based fuel tax schemes.

Italian organized crime families continue to maintain a powerful presence in Ontario and Quebec, and in Montreal a family within the Sicilian organization exerts influence over the other criminal organizations operating there. In April 2001, a $200 million Internet gambling operation allegedly linked to an Italian crime family was disrupted with arrests in Ontario and Quebec. Leaders of the Caruana family were sentenced in 2000 with the wrap-up of "Project Omerta." Despite these successes, however, authorities believe that IOC groups remain a significant threat and serious challenge for law enforcement in Canada.[65]

Aboriginal Organized Crime

Criminal organizations flourish in certain Canadian aboriginal communities, especially on the U.S.-Canada border where the smuggling of liquor, tobacco, and firearms is prevalent. In September 1997, on the Mohawk Kahnawake Reserve south of Montreal, the Royal Commission on Aboriginal Peoples seized machine guns and semi-automatic weapons that were part of a black market operation that sold firearms, explosives, drugs, cigarettes, and alcohol. Violence and political unrest on the reserves is an ongoing problem, as the Canadian government and the aboriginal peoples clash over taxation, logging rights, land claim settlements, redress for grievances, and a government aid package. Canadian authorities continue to fear that aboriginal smugglers will exploit the political situation for criminal gain.

Aboriginal street gangs in the prairie provinces of Western Canada are growing and forging alliances with other organized crime groups. The most powerful street gang is called the Manitoba Warriors and is involved in drug trafficking and prostitution. Members of the Warriors and the Indian Posse participated in a riot at Manitoba's Provincial Jail in April 1996 that caused $3 million in damage to the institution.

Authorities predict that aboriginal groups will continue to consolidate their control of prostitution and drugs in urban centers like Winnipeg.[66]

Outlaw Motorcycle Gangs (OMGs)

In 1996, the CISC concluded that Canada was plagued by 35 outlaw motorcycle gangs, with more than 70 chapters and 1,200 members. Since that time, the number of gangs, chapters, and members has increased dramatically. OMGs are involved in money laundering, murder, theft, counterfeiting, loan-sharking, extortion, prostitution, strip clubs, the illegal sale of alcohol, and the traffic in illegal firearms, stolen goods, alcohol, and cigarettes. The Hell's Angels are the largest and most powerful of the motorcycle clubs and, in addition to the aforementioned activities, are heavily involved in the importation and distribution of cocaine, the cultivation and exportation of marijuana (especially high-grade product grown in hydroponic labs), the production and distribution of methamphetamine and LSD, and traffic in synthetic drugs such as ecstasy.

The expansion of Hell's Angels chapters throughout the provinces of Canada has been explosive. The 1996 report from the CISC identified eleven Hell's Angels chapters—five in British Columbia, five in Quebec, and one in Nova Scotia. The 2001 report from the CISC noted that the Hell's Angels had established three chapters in Alberta, one in Manitoba, and one in Saskatchewan, and had added two additional chapters in British Columbia. The most dramatic expansion occurred in late 2000 and 2001 in Ontario, where the Angels established eleven chapters, formed an affiliated chapter (the Nomads), and developed prospect chapters in Niagara Falls and London. The 2001 Annual Report from the Organized Crime Agency of British Columbia observed that as of 2001, Canada had a total of thirty Hell's Angels chapters (up from just eleven in 1996) with some 500 members.[67]

Canadian law enforcement officials and intelligence gatherers have noted that OMGs commonly forge alliances with other biker gangs and organized crime groups, especially Asian and Italian-based syndicates (the Hell's Angels are closely aligned with the Quebec-based Rizzuto crime family). An ongoing trend seems to be the absorption of less powerful biker clubs into more powerful, transnational OMGs like the Hell's Angels and Bandidos.

Still, relationships among OMGs in Canada are not always cooperative. A biker war between the Hell's Angels and the Rock Machine that began in 1994 was ongoing as of late 2001. Sparked largely by competition over the drug trade in and around Montreal, by the end of 1998 the war had resulted in 103 homicides, 124 murder attempts, 9 missing persons, 84 bombings, and 130 incidents of arson. An October 2000 truce was short-lived, as sporadic violence between the rival gangs continued through 2001.[68]

Law enforcement in Canada has had some success against OMGs. Begun in 1995 as a result of the Hell's Angels–Rock Machine conflict, Operation Carcajou (Wolverine) centered in Montreal and subsequent spin-off regional squads came together in a coordinated investigation by 1999. The nationwide police efforts culminated on March 28, 2001, when the largest one-day police operation of its kind in Canadian history was launched against the Hell's Angels in Quebec, resulting in 138 arrests. Two days later an associated strike in Alberta brought about the arrest of fifty-one members and associates of the Calgary chapter of the Hell's Angels. Other positive results from "Operation Springtime 2001" and "Operation Shadow" included the seizure of 20 buildings worth $12 million, as well as the confiscation of $2.6 million in cash, 70 firearms (including two "cobra guns" and a rocket launcher), 120 kilograms of hashish, and 10 kilograms of cocaine.

Despite law enforcement successes, OMGs in Canada are expected to continue their expansion. Along with a myriad of independent and semiautonomous clubs in every province and reaching into the arctic, transnational gangs like the Hell's Angels and Bandidos are proliferating and forging alliances with other transnational crime groups. With chapters in twenty-six countries around the world, the Hell's Angels in particular will continue to make extensive use of financial networks to launder their illicit proceeds and play a leading role in transnational criminal enterprises based in Canada.[69]

CHAPTER 3

Smuggling, Transnational Theft, and "Eco-Crime"

Mats Berdal and Monica Serrano of the International Institute for Strategic Studies have said that the "iconic image," that symbol that best characterizes the threat of transnational organized crime, is not an airplane or a tank or even a gun, but a container. The use of standardized containers for shipping is very efficient, allows companies to substantially reduce inventories, and accounts for about 90 percent of the world's traded cargo by value. Unfortunately, smugglers have found the use of large shipping containers to be equally beneficial, using them to transport a broad range of contraband, from drugs and weapons to stolen automobiles and illegal migrants. Moreover, the sheer volume of world trade confounds law enforcement. Just as with laundered money hidden among trillions of legally wired funds, discovering contraband hidden in cargo containers is like "finding a needle in a haystack." A 2002 article in *The Economist* suggests that U.S. customs inspectors examine only 2 percent of inbound containers (about 9 million per year), often after the carriers have already traveled great distances.[1]

The increased use of sealed containers has manifested itself in the smuggling of illicit drugs. In the late 1970s and 1980s, traffickers used small private planes and speedboats to move contraband from South America and the Caribbean into Florida. Today, sealed shipping containers are more often used to ship large quantities of drugs at low cost and with minimal law enforcement risk. Even when inspectors do find a shipment, there is no clear culprit and criminal investigations are long and cumbersome. The use of cargo containers to ship illegal migrants into the United States has also been a growing problem.

The problem of securing U.S. borders against traffickers in contraband, including weapons of mass destruction, is enormous and perhaps insurmountable. In 1999, 125 million vehicles and 21.4 million import shipments entered the United States through 3,700 terminals in 301 ports of entry. The U.S. border with Mexico is the country's busiest entry point and the busiest land crossing in the world. In 1998, 278 million people, 86 million cars, and 4 million trucks and railcars entered the United States from Mexico. While legitimate trade with Mexico doubled in the 1990s, the movement of illicit drugs increased as well. In 1998, an estimated 60 percent of the cocaine and 29 percent of the heroin sold in the United States was imported from Mexico, a nation that is also a leading supplier of marijuana and methamphetamines. Under trade liberalization (NAFTA, for example), Mexican trucks, the vast majority of which are not inspected for content, may travel freely throughout the United States and Canada, enhancing legitimate and illegal commerce. It follows that a serious crackdown on drug shipments from Mexico necessarily translates into a significant burden for legitimate U.S.-Mexico trade.[2]

DRUG TRAFFICKING

One of the most pervasive of all criminal enterprises is the global narcotics trade, estimated to be a $500 billion a year industry. In the United States, limiting illicit drug importation, distribution, and use has proved to be extremely difficult. Success in weakening the Colombian Medellin cocaine cartel merely precipitated the rise of the Cali cartel and Mexican traffickers. Drug organizations in Mexico are now thought to control the supply of 70 percent of the cocaine, 80 percent of the foreign grown marijuana, and 80 percent of the raw methamphetamine ingredients consumed in the United States. Colombian groups have taken over the U.S. heroin market from Asia, moving a nearly 100 percent pure product through the Caribbean.[3]

On a global scale, the supply of heroin, cocaine, and cannabis continues to increase. The number of countries reporting cannabis seizures increased by a third between 1980 and 1994. Similarly, heroin and cocaine during the same period witnessed a rapid and consistent diffusion around the world. The reasons for the growth in the transnational drug trade are many and include the opening of new markets as well as technological, socioeconomic, and political changes that operate in tandem with the process of "globalization" to foster the industry. Advances in agriculture, such as hydroponics, new fertilizers, and selective breeding, increase coca, opium poppy, and cannabis yields per hectare, while the increased trade in legal precursor chemicals, improved scientific equipment, new extraction techniques, and chemical product diversification have resulted in the proliferation of new psychoactive drugs, including the popular MDMA (ecstasy). Socioeconomic and political changes are important factors as well. For example, increases in migration, shipping, aviation, communications, and a general liberalization of trade policies provide cover and new markets for traffickers. Finally, and perhaps most significantly, the proliferation of transnational drug trafficking is driven by an increase in the global demand for illicit drugs.[4]

The 2003 National Drug Control Strategy notes that there are five principal illegal drug markets in the United States: (1) there are 20 million users of marijuana in the United States who consume 10,000 metric tons grown domestically and more than 5,000 metric tons imported from Mexico and Canada; (2) 250 metric tons of cocaine are manufactured in Colombia and shipped through Mexico and the Caribbean to 5 million American users; (3) 1 million users of heroin are supplied by 13 metric tons of heroin manufactured in Mexico, Asia, and Colombia and shipped via commercial air and maritime carriers; (4) between 106 and 144 metric tons of methamphetamine are manufactured in Mexico and the United States and marketed to 1.3 million users; and (5) 8 metric tons of Ecstasy manufactured in Belgium and the Netherlands are shipped via commercial carriers to 3 million U.S. consumers.[5]

Cocaine from South America is shipped to the United States in elongated "go-fast" boats that carry about a ton of cocaine and in commercial fishing vessels that carry multiton loads. About half of the 500 or so major shipments annually that depart Colombia leave from its north coast destined for the Greater Antilles and Central America—the other half is shipped from the West Coast to Mexico. Once Colombian drugs are handed over to Mexican traffickers, typically the Mexican organizations take as much as 40 percent of the load in exchange for guaranteeing reimbursement to the Colombians if a shipment is lost. The U.S. government therefore seeks cooperation from the Colombian government to interdict the shipments in Colombian coastal waters before the Mexicans insure the contraband. Colombia has also grown through the 1990s to be a significant supplier of heroin to U.S. consumers. From almost no cultivation in 1990 to the present 6,500-hectare crop, Colombian-grown opium poppies produce about 4.3 metric tons of high-purity heroin to the U.S. market. The DEA has subsequently created a heroin task force in Colombia. Drug profits in Colombia also fuel that country's terrorist organizations—principally ELN, FARC, and AUC rebels. Terrorists killed more than 3,000 people in Colombia in 2001. Under President Uribe, Colombia's drug control program has been accelerated to include a tripling of the number of hectares sprayed between 1999 and 2002. The Bush White House has stated in its 2003 Drug Control Strategy that the U.S. Agency for International Development will devote resources to coca farmers displaced by increased spraying.

While efforts to increase the costs to traffickers in Colombia may have increased, the outlook is less favorable in Bolivia and Peru. Expanded drug control in Colombia, rising demand for cocaine in Europe and Latin America, and economic slumps have placed stress on legitimate public officials and provided the impetus for an increase in coca cultivation. Peru has reduced funding for drug control programs and weakened security in drug cultivation regions, especially those areas frequented by the terrorist organization Sendero Luminoso. Economic troubles have precipitated violent protests in Bolivia in recent years, emboldening radicals with a prococa agenda of supplying cocaine to the world market. From 2001 to 2002, Bolivian coca cultivation increased by 23 percent.

Renewed efforts by the Vincente Fox administration in Mexico to combat narcotics trafficking have met with violent resistance. In February 2001, masked men armed with machine guns herded fifteen men and boys into the back of a truck and killed twelve. In November of the same year, two federal judges and the wife of another judge were cut down by AK-47 fire from a passing vehicle—one judge had angered traffickers with an unfavorable ruling. Still, since Fox took office in 2000, fourteen major traffickers have been arrested in Mexico. In March 2002, a major blow was struck to the Tijuana-based Arellan Felix organization when Benjamin Arellano-Felix was arrested and his brother Ramon was killed. Other major arrests were made of Gulf cartel members, including that group's second in command and the leader of a Juarez-based gang who coordinated shipments. The Fox administration also has attacked public corruption in government and the military, arresting dozens of individuals in the fall of 2002 for aiding the drug trade and leaking information to traffickers.

The National Drug Control Strategy 2003 acknowledged the increase in opium poppy cultivation following the U.S. invasion and the fall of the Taliban regime. In 2002, Afghanistan had the distinction of becoming the world's largest opium producer once again, doubling the output of the world's other major opium producer, Burma (Myanmar).[6]

ARMS TRAFFICKING

The traffic in armaments is perhaps the most profitable of organized criminal endeavors and is intimately linked to the illicit drug trade. The Ninth

United Nations Congress on the Prevention of Crime and the Treatment of Offenders stated in a recent report:

> There is abundant evidence that organized crime is involved in the illegal arms trade and subversive activities that tamper with the rule of law in different parts of the world. The weight of the evidence indicates that it contributes to the political turmoil and upheaval occurring throughout the world. Drugs for weapons deals have become common in the world of organized crime, and many ethnic and political conflicts are aggravated by this unholy alliance.[7]

Armaments trafficking is complicated by the fact that the distinction between the legal and illegal supply of arms is not always clear. Transactions that may begin as legal nevertheless circumvent the law because the end user is either a "rogue state that the international community is trying to isolate" or perhaps an ethnic group attempting to circumvent an arms embargo. Sometimes quasi-licit and illegal arms trafficking is sanctioned by nation-states. For example, Great Britain violated its own laws when it allowed Matrix Churchill to sell advanced machine tools to Saddam Hussein prior to the Gulf War and tacitly approved weapons sales to both sides in the Iran-Iraq War. The link between the legitimate production and distribution of arms and transnational war profiteers is embodied by events in Yugoslavia in the early 1990s. In that war, Croatian Anton Kikas developed alliances with manufacturers of conventional ordnance in South Africa and with a powerful member of the Russian Mafiya, Aleksandr Kutzin. Kutzin chartered Boeing 707s to fly the conventional weaponry to Croatia, then used the same planes to transport nuclear cargo from former Soviet bloc countries to Zagreb, Yugoslavia.[8]

The illicit traffic in weapons is especially serious in Russia:

> Weapons, munitions, and other equipment are stolen from storage sites by civilian criminals, often in collusion with military sentries and other service personnel. Facilities are also successfully attacked or breached by criminal groups that neutralize or kill sentries and seize arms. . . . In addition, weapons are sold outright, individually and in lots of varying sizes, by officers and other military personnel stationed in Russia and abroad.[9]

Russian organized crime expert Louise Shelley has noted that a significant illicit trade in military equipment has supported armed conflicts in the former Soviet Republics and elsewhere throughout the world.[10] Moreover, lax security on Russia's stockpile of chemical, biological, and nuclear weapons is a serious concern, as international terrorists covet these materials.

Russia has the world's largest stockpile of chemical weapons—40,000 metric tons—as well as 25,000 nuclear warheads, 600 metric tons of weapons grade nuclear material, and an extensive biological weapons infrastructure. A recent investigation by U.S. General Accounting Office investigators found at some Russian sites that dangerous pathogens were stored in rooms secured by small padlocks and doorjambs sealed with wax and string. At another site, concrete security walls were crumbling to pieces. In the post-Soviet era, the United States has aided Russia in securing its weapon sites, but in recent years Moscow has grown reluctant to grant full access, thus hampering security efforts.[11]

In 2000, America's First International Crime Threat Assessment detailed the problem of arms trafficking further:

> The U.S. Government estimates that military equipment worth several hundred million dollars is sold annually on the illegal arms market to countries under UN arms embargoes. Insurgents, terrorists, and organized criminal groups acquire smaller quantities of small arms and other light infantry weapons on the illegal arms market.

The 2000 Threat Assessment observed that most arms sales are through the "gray market," where individual brokers and their firms exploit legitimate export licensing processes and falsify paperwork to disguise the nature of the goods, the recipient, and the supplier. In recent conflict in the former Yugoslavia and Afghanistan gray market, arms suppliers donated or sold tens of millions of dollars worth of weapons disguised as humanitarian aid. Purely "black market" arms transfers usually involve smaller quantities stolen from military stocks or gun stores. Traditional organized crime groups, such as Italian and Russian criminal organizations, have become increasingly involved in weapons smuggling since the end of the Cold War.[12]

ALIEN SMUGGLING AND TRAFFICKING IN PEOPLE

Trafficking in people has several transnational criminal dimensions, including alien smuggling, whereby foreign persons willingly contract with criminals to be smuggled into nations in Western Europe and North America, and trafficking in human beings, where people, especially women and children, are deceived or coerced into being transported across national borders for the purposes of prostitution, forced labor, and outright slavery. Authorities believe that criminal organizations are smuggling as many as 1 million people a year from poor to wealthier nations—a business estimated to yield $3.5

billion annually. As of 1996, the Immigration and Naturalization Service (INS) estimated that there were as many as 5 million undocumented illegal aliens living in the United States, the majority coming from Mexico and Central America.[13]

Criminal organizations that specialize in illegal immigrations operate with near impunity—only a few recipient countries like the United States have criminalized the practice. Moreover, the business of alien smuggling is made possible by the corruption of immigration officials in Belize, Guatemala, the Dominican Republic, and the United States. In recent years, the smuggling of Chinese people to Western countries such as the United States has received the most attention. Since January 1993, the U.S. Coast Guard has intercepted eleven different ships carrying some 2,100 illegal Chinese, and in January and June 2000, a total of sixty-one illegal Chinese immigrants were found dead inside cargo containers in Seattle and Britain. Still, authorities believe that Chinese migrants comprise only 20 percent of those in a global pipeline that stretches from China, India, Iraq, Iran, Pakistan, Romania, Sri Lanka, the Sudan, and on to Latin American countries and recipient countries in Europe and the United States. Standard fees charged by alien smugglers range from a few hundred dollars for Central Americans to more than $40,000 for Chinese nationals. At present, Central America has emerged as the principal gateway for U.S.-bound illegal migrants from around the globe. The transnational alien smuggling networks themselves are difficult to disrupt because they are composed of loose and far-flung associations of smugglers and escorts, fraudulent document vendors, complicit airline and bus company employees, and corrupt public officials from source and recipient nations.[14]

An insidious relationship exists between the demand for smuggling services and the need for laborers in the commercial sex industry. Trafficking in women and children for the purpose of prostitution and pornography is a global problem, and while many migrants are transferred to foreign lands with the full knowledge that they are to work as prostitutes, other highly vulnerable people indebted to smugglers are forced into sexual slavery. The U.S. government estimates that 700,000 women and children are transported across national boundaries every year, while the global prostitution industry is thought to generate at least $4 billion for transnational criminals. Since the early 1990s, there has been considerable growth in the trafficking of women from Eastern Europe to Western Europe, where as many as 500,000 foreign women work as prostitutes. Women from Eastern Europe and the former Soviet bloc are smuggled to the United States, Nigerians and Albanians are shipped to Italy, Thai women are shipped to Japan, and

Dominican women are smuggled into and work as prostitutes in Austria, Curacao, Germany, Greece, Haiti, Italy, the Netherlands, Panama, Puerto Rico, Spain, Switzerland, and Venezuela. Traffickers in women and children sometimes operate through ostensibly reputable employment agencies, travel agencies, marriage agencies, and entertainment companies.

The growth in global tourism, fear of AIDS, and the exploitation of computer networks by pedophiles drives the demand for child prostitutes. Transnational criminals have met the demand, exploiting migrants and purchasing children from desperate and impoverished parents. The United Nations reported in 1996 that child prostitution is very profitable and involves "highly organized syndicated networks." Estimates of the number of children used for the purpose of commercial sex include 650,000 in the Philippines, 200,000 in Thailand, 400,000 in India, 2,000,000 in Brazil, and 300,000 in the United States. The problem is present and growing in Benin, Nigeria, Senegal, Sudan, Kenya, Ghana, the Ivory Coast, Burkina Faso, Argentina, Bolivia, Chile, Colombia, Ecuador, Mexico, Peru, Nepal, Bangladesh, and Sri Lanka. Authorities report that children as young as five years old have been prostituted in Sicily.[15]

THE TRAFFIC IN HUMAN ORGANS

Human organs are a scarce and precious commodity and, for this reason, a black market exists. Trafficking in human organs and the exportation of organs utilizing false documents has been confirmed in Argentina, Brazil, Honduras, Mexico, and Peru, in most cases with Swiss, German, and Italian buyers. Cases have been documented in which doctors fabricated brain scans, declared patients brain dead, and then removed their corneas. In February 1992, Argentina's Minister of Health announced that blood and organs had been removed from the inmates of a mental hospital. The Naples-based Camorra places Mexican, Thai, and European children into secret clinics to have organs removed, and in Honduras, handicapped children are legally adopted and then sold like "spare parts." A Guatemalan police official has claimed that children in that country are sold to Americans as organ donors for $20,000.[16] Organ trafficking is apparently quite prevalent in Russia:

> One investigative report found one company that had extracted 700 major organs, kidneys, hearts and lungs, over 1,400 liver sections, 18,000 thymus organs, 2,000 eyes, and over 3,000 pairs of testicles. Moreover, one Moscow forensic detective saw these activities as being firmly under the control of organized crime, which he suggested had elaborate criminal structures for kid-

napping children and adults, using their organs for transplants and for medical experiments.[17]

The "419" criminal syndicates in Nigeria have also been involved in the selling of body parts. In the fall of 1996, the police arrested a local public official and hotel owner in the city of Owerri after they discovered heads, livers, kidneys, and genitalia in the hotel's freezer. Later, sixteen headless corpses were exhumed near the official's home. The Nigerian newspapers report that the traffic in body parts has been ignored in Nigeria for years because political and social elites have been involved in the lucrative trade.[18] In Juarez, Mexico, where the apparent serial homicide of at least ninety-one women has occurred over the last decade, Mexican authorities floated the theory in early 2003 that at least fourteen of the women may have been killed for the purpose of selling their body organs.[19]

TRANSNATIONAL THEFT

Organized theft is perhaps the most widespread of all criminal endeavors. The National Cargo Security Council has estimated that the losses due to air, ocean, and trucking cargo theft exceeded $30 billion from 1992 to 1994. In fact, researchers estimate that 90 percent of the dollar value of all objects that are stolen are pilfered by professional hijacking and burglary rings. Automobile theft is a multibillion dollar global industry with established international dimensions. Stolen vehicles are moved out of the United States inside shipping containers on huge cargo ships for destinations around the world. In 1996, a congressional committee looked into the activities of Russian criminals who export cars from the United States to the Russian republics. Many vehicles are stolen in New York City, driven to Chicago, hidden in containers, and shipped to former Soviet countries where they sell for three times their American value. Other criminal networks operating from the United States export stolen vehicles to Venezuela, Ecuador, the Dominican Republic, and Mexico. Luxury cars in Hong Kong are stolen and transported to China on motor boats. The problem is also extensive in Africa and Europe—automobile thefts tripled in Europe between 1989 and 1993.[20] The Chicago Crime Commission reported in 1997 that "if auto theft was legal, it would be number 50 on the Fortune 500 list."[21]

Art theft is also an extremely lucrative transnational criminal enterprise. Formed in 1991, the Arts Loss Register in London immediately compiled a database of 650,000 stolen art objects, to which 2,000 new items are added each month. Forty thousand pieces are stolen monthly in Great Britain alone.

In Russia and the former Soviet satellites, art galleries are looted and valuable objects shipped by train to Europe through Warsaw and Budapest. Fifteen thousand art objects valued at $32 million have been listed as stolen from the Czech Republic alone. During the war in Yugoslavia in 1991 and 1992, Serbian military forces looted forty-two art galleries, nine archives, and twenty-two libraries in Croatia. Worldwide, the value of paintings and fine art stolen is estimated at over $4 billion annually.[22]

Piracy on the high seas is not an anachronism, but a contemporary reality. Since the late 1980s, maritime crime has increased dramatically. The Strait of Malacca and the Phillip Channel south of Singapore have become especially dangerous for merchant ships, as have many of the waters around Thailand, Macao, Indonesia, China, and Hong Kong. In Brazil, shipping attacks have occurred in territorial waters and in port, and in March 1998, a Pakistani was killed off Somalia's northeastern coast when his ship was attacked by several boats equipped with machine guns. Aside from the routine acts of boarding and robbing, so-called "phantom ships" sail under faked documents or change their identity while at sea, then sell their cargo to either unknowing or uncaring customers. The Regional Piracy Center (RPC), established in Kuala Lumpur, issues daily status reports on the most dangerous shipping areas and acts as a clearinghouse for all reports of piracy. The RPC reports show that, through the mid-1990s, the number of incidents of piracy increased every year, while noting that the majority of incidents go unreported. In 1999, 408 crewmembers were taken hostage in ship boardings that involved 285 attacks on ships at sea or in port, a 25 percent increase from 1998. While piracy in U.S. coastal waters is rare, global piracy nevertheless has a significant impact. Pirates threaten sea trade lanes and international maritime commerce, raise insurance rates, and endanger navigation by leaving vessels under way but not in command. The U.S. Coast Guard has estimated that direct financial losses as a result of piracy on the high seas are about $450 million per year. While pirate groups appear to operate independently, some may be linked to more "traditional" organized crime groups. The International Maritime Bureau has uncovered strong evidence of Chinese syndicate involvement in many maritime frauds.[23]

Computer-related thefts have become increasingly common. Commercial activity conducted over the Internet and the large amounts of sensitive information on the Web have created new opportunities for thieves who pilfer social security numbers and credit card numbers. Software piracy and the theft of computers and computer components are highly profitable enterprises as well. Computers and components are easy to sell, maintain a high black market value, and are difficult to trace. Central processing units manufactured by the Intel Corporation are used as currency in certain parts of Mexico.[24] (More on "identity thefts" and related financial crimes in Chapter 4.)

ENVIRONMENTAL CRIMES

In 2000, America's first International Crime Threat Assessment reported that environmental crime is one of the fastest growing and most lucrative transnational criminal enterprises. Many of these crimes have a devastating effect on the natural environment. The illegal disposal of hazardous wastes by organized crime groups has been well documented, while both the export of toxic wastes to developing countries and a thriving black market in chlorofluorocarbons (CFCs) emerged in the 1980s and 1990s. The rising cost of legal disposal in rich industrialized nations and liberalized international trade policies have spawned a burgeoning North to South trade in hazardous wastes, much of which is illegal. Moreover, international environmental treaties meant to protect the environment have instead exacerbated the problem. Initiatives like the Basel Convention did not stop the export of hazardous wastes to the third world but did precipitate a "moderate" black market in waste exports. Similarly, the illegal trade in CFCs has exploded in direct response to the Montreal Protocol's production and consumption control rules. The smuggling of CFCs, commonly used as a refrigerant in cooling systems, is believed to contribute to the depletion of the ozone layer. Under the Montreal Protocol of 1996, the United States and other nations agreed to phase out CFC production and ban CFC imports. A thriving black market immediately developed because CFCs are still legally produced abroad and are commonly used in older machines not adaptable to other coolants. Authorities estimate that 20 million pounds of CFCs are smuggled every year. A recent law enforcement effort called Operation Cool Breeze led to forty-four convictions and seizures of more than 1.9 million pounds of CFCs valued at $30 million. The UN estimates that the global black market for ozone-depleting substances ranges from 20,000 to 30,000 metric tons annually, with half of that entering the United States. Criminal organizations are thought to earn an additional $10 billion to $12 billion per year by illegally dumping garbage and hazardous waste materials. Criminals take advantage of the billion dollar trade in recyclable materials, such as scrap metal, to commingle and ship waste in "trash-for-cash" schemes to countries in Europe, Asia, and Africa where disposal costs are low and regulations few. Companies

hired by Italian organized crime groups, like the 'Ndrangheta, dump radioactive wastes from Austria, France, and Germany into the Mediterranean
and Adriatic Seas.[25]

The theft and illicit traffic in natural resources earns transnational crime
groups $5 billion to $8 billion per year. Illegal logging and the trade in forest timber is rampant and well organized by crime syndicates in Africa, Eastern Europe, Latin America, China, and Southeast and Southwest Asia.
Russian crime groups earn some $4 billion annually from the illegal export
of 2 million metric tons of seafood, much of it to Japan. In 1997, Japan said
that it imported from Russia $1 billion worth of fish—six times the volume
Russia said that it exported. The poaching of sturgeon from the Caspian Sea,
as well as the illegal overharvesting of other significant species endangers the
existence of those species and their ecosystems.[26]

The illegal trade in exotic plants and animals is a massive global industry. In 1996, authorities estimated that between $10 billion and $20 billion in exotic life forms were traded illegally, with the United States leading
the list of purchasers. Fish and Wildlife officer Tom Striegler explains the
attraction: "A padded vest studded with 40 eggs from Australia's endangered black palm cockatoo, each worth $10,000, is far easier to smuggle
than an equal-valued cache of cocaine, simply because custom officials
aren't looking for cockatoo eggs." Snakes and tortoises are especially popular because of their ability to survive long trips, but the trade is no way
limited and includes all manner of species living and dead: Brazilian mon-
keys, Australian birds, the horns of endangered black rhinos, the bones of
tigers, elephant tusks, and exotic skins used for designer clothing are all
illegally harvested, smuggled, and sold on a global black market. Scientists
have said that the decimation of animals and their habitats could lead to
the collapse of entire ecosystems.[27]

The cultivation of illicit crops like coca and the opium poppy has serious
environmental consequences, including deforestation and soil and water
pollution. Slash and burn techniques for clearing land contributes to deforestation and soil erosion. In Peru, increased coca cultivation in the Upper
Huallaga Valley is responsible for the stripping of 1 million hectares of tropi-
cal forest resources. Refiners of heroin and cocaine dump toxic chemicals and
other waste by-products into countless streams and rivers, or else they bury
it in the ground, contaminating the soil and groundwater sources. Each year
in Colombia, 20 million liters of ethyl ether, acetone, ammonia, sulphuric
acid, and hydrochloric acid used to produce cocaine are dumped from jungle
laboratories into the headwaters of the Amazon and Orinoco rivers. In the

Huallaga Basin, few fish are left, and many of those remaining are unfit for consumption. In addition to exterminating or mutating entire species, agro-chemicals decrease the quality of potable water and present a substantial health threat to native populations.[28]

CHAPTER 4

Money Laundering and Other Financial Crimes

Perhaps the key to controlling transnational organized crime is cutting off the flow of illegal profits to those criminal entities. Authorities have estimated that $300 billion in illicit funds are laundered each year through a variety of financial and nonfinancial institutions and across national boundaries. Money laundering is not limited to drug trafficking activities, but is associated with nearly all types of for-profit criminality, including tax evasion, capital flight from one country to another, securities law violations, government covert operations, and the smuggling of contraband. Consider the following anecdotes:

- The Spence money laundering network of twenty-four individuals included a New York City police officer, two lawyers, a stockbroker, an assistant bank manager at Citibank, two rabbis, a firefighter, the honorary consul-general for Bulgaria, and two banks in Zurich. In this scheme, a trucking firm and beer distributorship served as fronts while a law firm guided the operation. Drug money was transported by couriers (including the rabbis, the firefighter, and the Bulgarian diplomat) and by Federal Express to a New York City trucking business. The lawyers subsequently placed the money into various bank accounts with the assistance of the Citibank assistant manager. The money was then wired to various accounts in Europe, including a private bank in Switzerland. Bankers on that end ensured that the money made its way to designated accounts for repatriation. Authorities estimated that between 1993 and 1994, the Spence group laundered $70 million to $100 million in drug proceeds.[1]

- In Operation Goldmine, police uncovered the operation of Speed Joyeros (speed jewelers), a Panamanian gold and jewelry business that launders narcotics money for Colombian traffickers. Officials seized 1.6 tons of finished gold jewelry and 2.3 tons of finished silver jewelry in this operation.[2]
- By May 2002, in Operation Oasis, police seized over $13 million in bulk under new Patriot Act provisions that gave the Customs Service exclusive investigatory jurisdiction over inbound and outbound smuggled bulk currency.[3]
- On March 14, 2002, a New York City police officer pled guilty to laundering $6 million to $10 million obtained from drug sales in the NYC region. Over a two-year period, it was determined that Colombian traffickers had shipped over sixty tons of cocaine to NYC. Drug money was picked up in $100,000 to $500,000 parcels and driven to Miami, where businesses accepted the cash in exchange for goods that were subsequently shipped to Colombia.[4]
- The DEA and the U.S. Attorney's Office for the Southern District of New York concluded a long-term investigation of the Khalil Kharfan organization, a sophisticated money laundering operation that funneled about $100 million in narcotics proceeds. The Colombia cell has staff stationed in Puerto Rico, Florida, New York, and New Jersey, while international businesses and banks in Panama, Israel, Switzerland, and Colombia used "members" to open fictitious businesses.[5]
- In January 2001, Citibank Miami filed a Suspicious Activity Report (SAR) in relation to the deposit of $15 million by Victor Alberto Venero-Garrido. The FBI subsequently arrested Venero and determined that he was the courier for the former chief of the Peruvian National Intelligence Service, Vladimiro Lenin Montesinos-Torres. Montesinos had fled Peru while under investigation for trafficking in narcotics, stealing government money, and violating human rights. Intelligence information revealed that Montesinos had generated over $450 million from defense contract kickbacks, gunrunning, embezzlement, and protection payments from drug traffickers that he laundered through a global network of front companies and bank accounts. When an associate of Montesinos attempted to extort $38 million (money that had been seized in the investigation) from U.S. bank officials, the subsequent investigation led to the arrest of Montesinos in Caracas, Venezuela.[6]
- In August 1998, an SAR alerted law enforcement to a series of large transfers from a Russian bank correspondent account to accounts in the Bank of New York. The FBI's Russian Organized Crime Task Force and the

U.S. Attorney's Office for the Southern District of New York subsequently investigated Peter Berlin and his wife, Ludmila Edwards, a Bank of New York account executive. Eventually authorities seized over $21.6 million from accounts at the Bank of New York, the correspondent account for a Russian bank at the Bank of New York, and several additional Berlin "entities." (Berlin and his wife eventually pled guilty to money laundering and related charges, forfeiting some $8.1 million).[7]

Money laundering is a criminal process that exemplifies the symbiotic relationships among legitimate and illicit businesspeople—although the demarcation between the two is not so distinct. In fact, with this activity the distinction between organized crime and white-collar crime becomes completely blurred, because the most important actors are typically accountants, tax lawyers, bankers, and public officials. The process of laundering funds involves three stages: (1) placement, or introducing cash into the banking system or into legitimate commerce; (2) layering, or separating the money from its criminal origins by passing it through a series of financial transactions; and (3) integration, the process of fusing the funds with legitimately obtained money or providing a plausible explanation for its ownership. The methods for laundering dirty money are numerous and include everything from physically smuggling large bundles of cash out of the United States to be placed in foreign bank accounts to concealing ill-gained profits among legitimate bank-to-bank wire transfers of aggregate funds. Wire transfers systems in particular provide criminal organizations with a swift and essentially risk-free method for moving and disguising illegal profits. The electronic movement of illicit funds is easily hidden among wire transfers moved by electronic funds transfers systems such as Fed Wire, the Clearing House for Interbank Payment Systems (CHIPS), and the Society for Worldwide Interbank Financial Telecommunication (SWIFT). Each day, Fed Wire and CHIPS move more than 465,000 wire transfers valued at over $2 trillion alone, while the total of laundered funds worldwide *per year* is estimated at only $1 trillion. In the United States, illicit transfers are easily hidden among the 700,000 mostly legitimate wire transfers that occur every day.[8]

Money launderers often use legitimate businesses as fronts or incorporate shell companies in foreign countries to provide an ostensible explanation for criminal proceeds. False invoicing is common as well: Greatly overpriced goods imported into the United States provide cover for large wire transfers abroad. Electronic money laundering often involves the complicity of bank officials, domestic and foreign. Launderers typically choose a "dollar economy" where U.S. dollars circulate freely (such as Panama and Hong

Kong), but especially enjoy countries with favorable tax and bank secrecy laws (such as the Cayman Islands, Switzerland, and Luxembourg).[9]

THE PROBLEM OF CORRESPONDENT BANKING

In correspondent banking, one bank provides services to another bank to move funds, exchange currencies, or carry out other financial transactions. The industry norm is for U.S. banks to have dozens, hundreds, and even thousands of correspondent relationships many with high-risk foreign banks. Through the correspondent accounts they provide to foreign banks, U.S. banks have become conduits for dirty money flowing into the U.S. banking system, thereby facilitating drug trafficking, financial frauds, and all manner of transnational organized crimes. Moreover, foreign banks can establish U.S. correspondent accounts with any bank that is authorized to do business in the United States even if the bank is not domiciled in the United States. Such accounts give clients and owners of poorly regulated and corrupt foreign banks with weak or nonexistent anti–money laundering controls direct access to the U.S. financial system.

In February 2001, the U.S. Permanent Subcommittee on Investigations issued a report of its findings on the problem of correspondent banking. Virtually every U.S. bank examined by U.S. congressional investigators had established accounts with offshore banks limited to transacting business with persons outside the licensing jurisdiction, and some had relationships with shell banks that had no physical presence in any country conducting business with their clients. The report concluded that money laundering oversight of correspondent accounts by U.S. banks is typically weak and ineffective. A notable failure is that U.S. banks are largely unaware to what extent their foreign bank clients allow third-party banks to use their U.S. correspondent accounts. High-risk foreign banks often gain access to the U.S. financial system by operating through U.S. correspondent accounts held by other foreign banks. During the course of the Permanent Subcommittee on Investigations hearings, many bank officials were seemingly surprised to learn that they were providing wire transfer services or handling Internet gambling deposits for foreign banks they had never heard of or with whom they had no direct relationship. To compound matters, foreign banks with U.S. correspondent accounts have special forfeiture protections under U.S. law, a vulnerability money launderers seem to be specifically targeting.

The following list includes some of the findings from the case histories developed by the congressional investigators:

- Laundering illicit proceeds and facilitating crime by accepting deposits or processing wire transfers involving funds that the high-risk foreign bank knew or should have known were associated with drug trafficking, financial fraud, or other wrongdoing;
- Conducting high-yield investment scams by convincing investors to wire-transfer funds to the correspondent account to earn high returns and then refusing to return any monies to the defrauded investors;
- Conducting advance-fee-for-loan scams by requiring loan applicants to wire-transfer funds to the correspondent account to earn high returns and then refusing to return any monies to the defrauded investors;
- Facilitating tax evasion by accepting client deposits, commingling them with other funds in the foreign bank's correspondent account, and encouraging clients to rely on bank and corporate secrecy laws in the foreign bank's home jurisdiction to shield the funds from U.S. tax authorities;
- Facilitating Internet gambling, illegal under U.S. law, by using the correspondent account to accept and transfer gambling proceeds.[10]

Specialized bank accounts practically invite misuse by professional money launderers. For example, "threshold accounts" are programmed to automatically wire funds to a foreign bank account when a designated level of deposits is reached. Foreign accounts could be "cupo" accounts that are permitted to receive a certain percentage of U.S. dollars—U.S. export-import companies commonly maintain cupo accounts in foreign countries and, for a fee, allow illegal profits to be wired overseas. Some foreign companies establish "payable-through accounts" that give their foreign customers signature authority to use the account to transact business in the United States. A single account may be used by thousands of individuals and by foreign banks, while the number of such accounts held by foreign banks and the number of customers who use those accounts is unknown.[11]

OTHER COMMON METHODS

Although banks have been the primary focus of attempts to control illegal wire transfers, there exist an estimated 200,000 nonbank money transmitters in the United States, ranging in size from Western Union to small neighborhood businesses. Money launderers have in fact adapted to strict regulation in the banking industry by developing new methods and by shifting their activities to money order firms (like Western Union, American Express, and MoneyGram), check-cashing services, trading companies, gold and precious metals dealers, foreign currency exchanges, insurers, mortgagors, brokers, importers, exporters, casinos, and express delivery services. Internet-based businesses are also convenient fronts for laundering money globally, and new banking practices, such as direct access banking and the use of "cybercurrrency" (microchip-based electronic money transferred via smart cards and the Internet), complicate attempts at law enforcement. The problem of detection and enforcement is compounded further by "underground" banking systems such as the "chit" system in China and the "hawala" in India and Pakistan.[12]

Informal parallel banking networks are based on trust, family ties, and regional ethnic and gang affiliations. Systems like the hawala practically guarantee anonymity and leave little or no trail for investigators. "Underground banking" systems such as these allow for the remittance of currency or other forms of monetary value, usually gold, without the burden of physical transportation or the use of contemporary monetary instruments. A typical hawala transaction, whereby funds are to be moved from the United Kingdom to India, involves providing the money to a "hawaladar," or hawala dealer, in the United Kingdom. Then the hawaladar contacts another hawaladar by phone or fax in India to request an equivalent sum minus a small commission to be paid in Indian rupees or gold to the individual designated by the customer in the United Kingdom. When accounts between hawaladars become unbalanced over time, the accounts are settled through reciprocal remittances, trade invoice manipulation, gold and precious gem smuggling, the conventional banking system, or the physical movement of currency. (Because the settlement of unbalanced accounts often involves reentry into traditional financial systems, officials believe that this stage is possibly the best stage for attack.) The U.S. government participated in a hawala conference in the United Arab Emirates in May 2002, a congress that resulted in the Abu Dhabi Declaration calling on all countries to regulate hawalas based on the Financial Action Task Force's (FATF) Special Recommendations on Terrorist Financing. The Financial Crimes Enforcement Network, or FinCEN, hosted a seminar for domestic law enforcement in May 2002 and sponsored an international training seminar in Mexico in October 2002 to develop and implement strategies for regulating alternative remittance systems such as hawalas.[13] (For more on the FATF and FinCEN, see Chapter 6.)

The growing number of technologies devised to transfer payments electronically, known by the generic term "digital cash," facilitates the sale of information over networks and fosters the growth of new businesses. However, digital cash also provides new opportunities for money launderers. The problem of smuggling bulk paper currency is eliminated: When millions of dollars can be stored on a "smart card" the size of a credit card, an entire year's worth of illicit profits can be transported quickly and securely in the criminal's wallet. Obviously, funds accumulated in one country can be instantaneously transferred and downloaded in another, rendering the present use of Currency Transaction Reports irrelevant (an electronic version of the CTR being the obvious law enforcement response). Growth in the use of electronic currency is sure to present profound difficulties for detecting and thwarting money laundering, as the movement of funds could virtually eliminate the need to use banks or other nonbank money transmitters (as with standard wire transfers) and provide a high level of anonymity for launderers.[14] Once illicit funds are converted to electronic currency, the money becomes virtually untraceable, and the criminal has full access from practically any computer terminal in the world.[15]

James R. Richards states that the nonbank money transmitter most synonymous with money laundering is the *casas de cambio*, peso-dollar exchange businesses that cropped up following the devaluation of the peso in 1982. Authorities have estimated that 80 percent of the more than 1,000 *casas de cambio* along the U.S.-Mexico border are involved in money laundering. The *casas* are largely unregulated and in many Latin and Central American countries serve as alternative banking systems. The typical *casa* charges between 2 percent and 5 percent for its laundering services and washes approximately $5 million per month—the largest is thought to launder some $200 million every six months. In Colombia, *casas de cambio* are called *giro* ("wire") houses.[16]

Another common laundering method is dollar discounting, whereby a drug trafficker or other criminal instructs his accountants to auction illicit proceeds at a discount to a broker—the broker assumes the risk of laundering the money. Typically, the money broker will approach a businessperson in Colombia or the Panama Free Zone who needs U.S. dollars to buy goods (or contraband) in the United States. The purchaser of the discounted dollars then deposits the discounted amount in pesos in the trafficker's Colombian account. The dollars are physically present in the United States and are obtained by the dollar purchaser through a variety of sophisticated schemes involving false bills of lading, invoices, and other methods; for example, the transaction may appear legitimate, but actually involves payment for fifty items when only ten are shipped.

Mirror image trading is the practice of buying contracts for one account while selling an equal number from another. Because both accounts actually belong to the same individual, profits or losses are netted. Of course, these transactions are hidden among millions of dollars worth of legitimate transactions. The Bank of Credit and Commerce International (BCCI) used mirror image trading in the commodities market to launder drug money for Panama's Manuel Noriega.

In a "reverse flip," a money launderer buys a property at a documented price well below the market value, paying the balance under the table to a complicit seller. The launderer then simply resells the property at its true value, realizing an ostensibly legal profit and effectively washing ill-gained revenue. Using inflated prices to pay for imported goods is among the most common of laundering methods. Money launderers work through front companies or accomplices to create false invoices for goods never purchased or bought at greatly inflated prices. A Florida International University analysis of Commerce Department data found that the fraudulent valuation of goods by international traders costs the United States $30 billion a year in lost tax revenue.

Casinos are now more carefully regulated, but have been and may continue to be effective money laundering vehicles. Testimony before the U.S. Senate includes the story of an organized crime figure who walked into an Atlantic City casino with $1.2 million in small bills weighing about 300 pounds. After some losses, the individual cashed in $800,000 worth of chips for $100 bills, weighing about 16 pounds. A few days later, the money was deposited in a Swiss bank—a simple but effective means of washing dirty money. James R. Richards states that the potential for money laundering through on-line casinos is "staggering." The latest version of Internet casinos use digital telephone technology and laptop computers, are located "offshore" where there are few if any regulations, and rely on encrypted electronic money payments—in short, detecting and controlling money laundering through such "virtual" means may be impossible.[17]

Greater regulation of banks has precipitated an increase in the use of insurance companies and securities dealers and brokers to launder funds. For example, launderers sometimes purchase a single premium annuity under a false name or through a shell corporation, then cancel the annuity with a small penalty. The insurance company issues a check for the balance, and the funds appear legitimate. James R. Richards describes a typical scheme:

> [T]he launderer will purchase or create a corporation in a country with little or no insurance regulations. That corporation will then purchase or create an insurance of reinsurance company, and create some sort of legitimate sales force in the U.S., being licensed to do so on the state level by the various state Commissioners of Insurance. Cash generated from criminal activities, such as drug distribution, is then funneled through various "placement" schemes and placed with the company as insurance premiums. The company creates a real-

istic audit trail to give the appearance of legitimacy. Then, false claims are filed and paid to the "insured" entities or individuals, who then can "integrate" these seemingly legitimate funds into the mainstream financial world.[18]

Launderers also commonly target securities dealers and brokers. In one infamous case, Drexel, Burnham, and Lambert investment banker Dennis Levine laundered over $13 million in insider trading profits through two Panamanian companies. Both E.F. Hutton and Merrill Lynch were involved in schemes to launder over $20 million in heroin money in the late 1980s. More recently, the grandson of Dean Witter pled guilty to attempting to launder over $1 million in drug profits, and in 1997, a Prudential Bache Securities stockbroker was convicted for laundering more than $2 million for nine suspected Colombian drug traffickers.[19]

RECENT MONEY LAUNDERING CASE STUDIES

On July 1, 1998, the chief officers of Supermail, Inc. were arrested on money laundering charges stemming from a joint two-year FBI–Los Angeles police department investigation dubbed "operation mule train." The company was one of the largest check cashing companies in the western United States and a leading money transfer agent that provided services to Mexico and Latin America. In the course of the investigation, undercover agents approached the manager of a company store in Reseda, California. The manager agreed to launder "drug money" for a fee, doing so by converting large amounts of cash into money orders. Corporate officers later authorized the issuance of more money orders and the wire transfer of large sums of money to a secret bank account in Miami. In all, the defendants laundered more than $3 million, and were sentenced variously to forty-six to seventy-two months in prison.[20]

Laundering drug proceeds is not the only activity engaged in by launderers, as increasingly the proceeds of "white-collar crimes" are moved beyond the reach of law enforcers. One example of a successful intervention, dubbed "Operation Risky Business," involved a 1994 advance fee scam whereby individuals placed ads in newspapers promising venture capital loans in exchange for up-front charges ranging from $50,000 to $2.2 million. After paying the fee, victims were asked to sign a contract requiring them to obtain a letter of credit ranging from $2 million to more than $20 million as collateral. When victims were unable to quickly obtain such large letters of credit, the scam artists said that they had violated their contract and forfeited their advance fee. The criminals incorporated Caribbean American Bank, Ltd. in Antigua and Barbuda to hide the money they had stolen. A joint Customs and FBI investigation discovered that numerous front companies and "the bank" (comprising eighteen "storefront operations") were used by the scam artists to purchase real estate, vehicles, yachts, and airplanes with the fraudulent proceeds. Some of the defendants issued themselves credit cards in the name of the front companies so that they could spend the stolen money on credit anywhere in the world. To date, Operation Risky Business resulted in the conviction of 19 people who defrauded over 400 individuals of at least $60 million.[21]

U.S. Customs, the DEA, and Colombian law enforcement arrested thirty-seven individuals in January 2002 as part of a two-and-one-half-year investigation of Colombian peso brokers who laundered drug money for the Colombian Gamboa or Caracol cartel. Peso brokers solicited undercover customs agents to pick up currency in New York, Chicago, Los Angeles, Miami, and San Juan and wire the proceeds to accounts in U.S. financial institutions. Typically, these accounts were in the name of Colombian companies or banks with correspondent accounts with a U.S. bank. Laundered funds were then withdrawn from Colombian banks in the form of Colombian pesos. Investigators seized over $8 million in cash, 400 kilos of cocaine, 100 kilos of marijuana, and 6.5 kilos of heroin.[22]

THE BLACK MARKET PESO EXCHANGE

The Black Market Peso Exchange (BMPE) is the largest known money laundering system in the Western Hemisphere—Colombian narcotics traffickers repatriate up to $5 billion annually using the BMPE. Typically, narcotics traffickers sell drugs in the United States for U.S. dollars and then sell the currency to the agent of a Colombian black market peso broker. Next, the U.S. currency is sold to Colombian importers, who purchase goods and ship them to Colombia. Essentially, the wholesale value of the cocaine or other drugs returns to Colombia in the form of trade goods (although some U.S. currency is simply smuggled in bulk back to Colombia).[23] James R. Richards summarizes this relatively complex money laundering system, called *la vuelta* or the "cycle": (1) A Colombian drug cartel exports cocaine to the United States; (2) The cocaine is sold for U.S. currency; (3) The cartel sells the cocaine proceeds in lots or blocks to brokers, launderers, and/or black market peso exchangers; (4) The broker or launderer begins the laundering cycle by placing, layering, and integrating the bulk currency into the U.S. financial and banking systems; (5) The U.S. dollars are sold to Colombian importers at a rate that reflects their savings on import and currency taxes and duties, but includes the costs of the illegality of the enterprise; (6) The importers purchase goods from the United States or elsewhere, using the U.S. dollars or dollar accounts; (7) The goods are imported to Colombia, where they are sold to Colombians for Colombian pesos.[24]

From March 1997 to May 1999, the Customs Service conducted a successful investigation (called "Operation Skymaster") involving the BMPE system. Undercover agents gained the confidence of Colombian peso brokers who were working for Colombian narcotics traffickers. The customs agents were directed to retrieve bulk cash drug money, which they wire-transferred to various government-controlled accounts. Using the Colombian BMPE, the peso brokers "exchanged" the dollars on deposit in the designated bank accounts for pesos obtained from Colombian importers of U.S. goods. The peso brokers then arranged to have the dollars wired to the bank accounts of U.S. exporters as payment for the goods received by the Colombian importers. Once the importers received confirmation that the dollar wire transfers were sent, they paid the peso brokers the equivalent amount in pesos. The final stage in the process occurred when the brokers delivered the pesos to the Colombian narcotics traffickers. As of 2001, Operation Skymaster had resulted in a dozen convictions and the initiation of civil forfeiture actions against the bank accounts that received the wire transfers.[25]

In a similar investigation, DEA, IRS, and the U.S. Attorney's office in Atlanta joined forces in "Operation Juno," an investigation in which undercover agents picked up drug proceeds in $100,000 to $500,000 parcels in cities across the United States as well as Madrid and Rome. Drug money was then wired to a secret bank account in Atlanta and redistributed to various accounts in the United States and around the world. Once again, the traffickers directed the undercover agents to use the BMPE to launder the funds. In December 1999, a federal grand jury in Atlanta indicted five individuals from Colombia and initiated civil forfeiture proceedings.[26]

IDENTITY THEFT AND OTHER FINANCIAL CRIMES

Frauds involving financial access devices are a growing problem. Credit cards, debit cards, smart cards, and communications systems that transfer financial data are used to steal billions of dollars globally. In just one year (1996), major credit card issuers estimated fraud losses in excess of $2 billion. Although Mexico has emerged as a center of counterfeit credit card manufacturing plants, the industry is global. For example, a recent counterfeit credit card suppression case in Guanzhuang, China, resulted in the confiscation of thousands of counterfeit credit cards, magnetic strips, issuer holograms, embossers, encoders, laptop computers, manufacturing equipment, and uncut blank credit cards. The scheme stretched from China to Honolulu, Bangkok, Hong Kong, Macau, Canada, Taiwan, and Buffalo, New York.

Identity theft involves the use of stolen information to obtain credit cards, apply for drivers' licenses, take out loans, and obtain foreign visas. The Justice Department says that stolen credit card numbers affect as many as 700,000 Americans each year.[27] Since the Federal Trade Commission started keeping data in 2000, the number of complaints related to identity theft has risen to 43 percent of total fraud reported—the 162,000 reported victims in 2002 was double the previous year's figure.[28] Some Russian crime groups skim credit card details and reencode them on plastic cards to be used in another country. Waiters in restaurants and hotels are known to skim magnetic-stripe cards and transmit information instantaneously to gang members overseas. Data can then be implanted on counterfeit blank plastic called "white-cards" and used to make cash advances or to purchase goods in multiple locations.[29] In January 2003, four H&R Block employees were charged with stealing the identities of over two dozen tax preparation customers. The accused stole names, addresses, social security numbers, and dates of birth in order to divert tax refunds and set up credit card accounts.[30]

Internet-based frauds also seem to be on the increase, with the FBI reporting a tripling in the number of complaints (48,252) from 2001 to 2002. The National White Collar Crime Center reports that the most common complaint in this area was Internet auction fraud, followed by nondelivery of purchased merchandise, credit card fraud, and fake investments/advance fee frauds.[31] In March 2003, the House Judiciary Committee heard testimony on the problem of on-line piracy—the placing of pirated movies, music, games, and software on the Internet. U.S. Deputy Assistant Attorney General John Malcolm testified that so-called "warez" groups compete with one another to obtain high quality free access to pirated digital materials. Although warez groups do not engage in piracy for monetary gain, other transnational criminals do steal intellectual property for the sole purpose of making money. The manufacture of optical disks that contain pirated software, movies, music, and video games is apparently most prevalent in Asia and parts of the former Soviet Union; however, the disks are distributed throughout the world, often through South and Central America and into the United States.[32] The Software Publishers Association has estimated that US$11 billion was lost in 1998 due to software piracy, with much of the theft perpetrated over the Internet. A total of US$15 billion to $17 billion is lost each year due to such copyright infringements.[33]

The exploitation and evasion of international trade laws, counterfeiting operations, and predatory trade practices are also serious transnational crime problems. By undercutting U.S. trade laws, international criminals pose a threat to international security and economic stability. Moreover, investigators have found that trade crime is often but one piece of a complex puzzle of international criminal offenses that include arms trafficking, drug trafficking, and money laundering. Improved copying and publishing technologies foster international counterfeiting operations and include the reproduction of financial instruments such as traveler's checks, money orders, and commercial checks. Transnational criminals increasingly use fictitious securities and negotiable instruments to defraud individuals, governments, corporations, and financial institutions. False financial instruments are used to underwrite loans, serve as insurance collateral, and defraud pension funds and retirement accounts. Counterfeiting and pirating U.S. goods endanger public safety and rob U.S. industry of billions of dollars in research, innovation, and artistic creation. American companies are thought to lose over $200 billion a year because of merchandise counterfeiting. Counterfeiting and copyright, trademark, and patent infringement distort markets and international trade, cause huge losses to domestic and foreign industries, and have been linked to organized crime groups and the financing of terrorist organizations. U.S. Customs uses the twenty-two Mutual Assistance Agreements it has with other countries to combat the flow of counterfeit merchandise into the United States. Customs also targets those who use the Internet to violate intellectual property rights. At the Cyber-Smuggling Center, customs officials investigate transnational syndicates that produce millions of pirated audio and video CDs, as well as pirated computer software.[34]

Unfair and predatory international trade practices are a serious transnational criminal problem as well. Many countries evade U.S. import quotas that threaten American job and earnings. The most common type of fraud in this area is illegal transshipment, which occurs when goods produced in a country subject to U.S. quotas are shipped through a third country not subject to the given trade quota. This practice is common with textiles, especially apparel. Since 1996, textile clearinghouses give U.S. Customs the ability to identify shipment trends and better target violators. Law enforcement has had some success stifling these violations of U.S. trade law. For example, in cooperation with the government of Hong Kong, U.S. authorities convicted thirty-nine factories for fraudulently obtaining Hong Kong export licenses. Similarly, Macau recently assessed penalties on fourteen factories that made false claims as to the origin of their goods in order to obtain textile visas.[35]

Industrial theft and economic espionage is a growing international crime that costs American companies an estimated $18 billion a year. Particularly troubling are foreign efforts to steal proprietary trade secrets and sophisticated technologies with military applications (such as ballistic missile guidance systems). President Clinton signed the Economic Espionage Act in 1996 in an effort to combat this problem. The law provided for penalties of up to fifteen years in prison and a $500,000 fine for each violation.[36]

Finally, advance-fee fraud is one of the most lucrative financial crimes worldwide. Criminals (often members of Nigerian "419" syndicates) pretend to be government officials, banking officers, and oil company executives when they mail or fax letters to individuals and businesses in the United States, luring investors with promises of huge windfalls. Of course, the targets are required to provide a large fee up front to cover the cost of taxes, legal fees, and bribes before the deal can be completed. Financial losses to U.S. citizens from such scams are in the hundreds of millions annually.[37]

CHAPTER 5

Terrorism and Weapons of Mass Destruction

Although terrorism as a tangible threat probably did not fully material-ize in the American psyche until after September 11, 2001, the problem is not new to the United States. As Jonathan R. White observed: "Domestic terrorism is older than the Republic." Nationalistic terrorism began during the frontier wars of the seventeenth century, while militant labor movements in post–Civil War America spawned revolutionary and repressionist terror. Vigilante groups operated in the United States in colonial times, and in the 1800s there were at least 300 separate vigilante movements. The FBI was tracking possible foreign terrorists as early as 1935.[1]

Domestic terrorist movements with both right-wing and left-wing ideolo-gies have been active in the United States in recent decades as well. The Symbionese Liberation Army was one of the great media events of the 1970s. That small cell kidnapped and brainwashed Patty Hearst, the granddaugh-ter of the publishing tycoon. The Black Panthers murdered scores of white police officers in the 1960s and 1970s, and the Weathermen bombed New York City police headquarters in 1970, the Capital Building in 1971, and the Pentagon in 1972. The most deadly and enduring campaigns of insur-gent terrorism in the United States has been aimed at independence for Puerto Rico. Two Puerto Rican nationalists tried to assassinate Harry Truman in 1950, and in 1954, five members of Congress were wounded when Puerto Rican nationals shot them from the gallery of the U.S. House of Representatives. Since 1970, Puerto Rican terrorist groups, such as Armed Forces for National Liberation (FALN), have initiated 370 acts of terrorism in which nineteen people have died. Anti-Castro Cubans have also been ac-tive in the United States since the early 1960s. Groups like Alpha 66 and

Omega 7 have at times been considered the most dangerous terrorist groups in the country. In 1975 alone, Omega 7 was responsible for thirty bombings. In recent years, so-called Christian Identity groups and white supremacists that advocate a race war have dominated right-wing terrorism in the United States. The militia movement is a 1990s phenomenon that heralded a resurgence of right-wing extremism typified by an ideology of race hatred, survivalism, and an opposition to government control.[2]

"Ecoterrorists" embrace the basic ideology of mainstream environmentalists (preservation of the planet), but differ in that they see Earth's salvation in the elimination of humankind, or at least the destruction of civilization as we know it. Although some forms of environmental extremism have existed for some time (Greenpeace destroyed property prior to 1977), radical ecoterrorism is a recent development and can be traced back to 1980 when five ecological militants formed Earth First. These extremists view human beings as no more important than animal and plant species, including viruses and bacteria, or for that matter, inanimate objects such as rivers and mountains. Earth First and like-minded militants engineered hundreds of assaults in the 1980s in which many people were injured and millions of dollars in property were destroyed. Bridges, transmission towers, electrical power transformers, and logging equipment has been dynamited and destroyed. In one of the more spectacular episodes, two ecoterrorists destroyed a pair of whaling vessels and a processing plant in Iceland in 1986. Environmental terrorism declined throughout the 1990s, perhaps the main reason being ideological dissent among the radicals. A related breed of exotic terrorists are the animal liberationists. The primary animal-rights terrorist group has been the Animal Liberation Front, which has been most active in Britain. In 1995, official statistics indicated 80 attacks per month in 1995, while the U.S. State Department indicated 313 such attacks over several years. Physical attacks, acts of arson, firebombings, and threats were directed against furriers, butchers, restaurants, veterinarians, zookeepers, abattoirs, and especially medical research facilities. In 1997, the Association of American Medical Colleges reported more than 3,700 acts of harassment by animal rights activists.[3]

THE EVOLUTION OF TERRORISM

Terrorism has evolved in the latter half of the twentieth century into forms more frightening than before. While flaws in human nature and the supply of madmen have not diminished, technological advances have made possible the killing of tens of thousands, perhaps hundreds of thousands of people in a single strike. In the past traditional terrorist movements had hundreds and sometimes thousands of members (some still do, such as the FARC in Colombia), but the new terrorist groups can be very small, consisting of a few people or even an individual. Terrorism Walter Laqueur notes that the smaller the group, "the more radical it is likely to be, the more divorced from rational thought, and the more difficult to detect."[4] Laqueur also observes that "fanaticism inspired by all kinds of religious-sectarian-nationalist convictions is now taking on a millenarian and apocalyptic tone," as well as "the rise of small sectarian groups that lack clear political or social agendas other than destroying civilization, and in some cases humankind."[5] Primarily groups concerned with influencing an audience to bring about political and social change once characterized terrorism; now, merely a desire to destroy life and create havoc drives many fanatics. Coupled with these extremist ideologies is the proliferation of weapons of mass destruction—nuclear, radiological, biological, and chemical.

WEAPONS OF MASS DESTRUCTION

Just four months prior to the September 2001 terrorist attacks upon the United States, staff at the Center for Strategic and International Studies (CSIS) compiled a threat assessment regarding weapons of mass destruction. In their report, the CSIS staff created four scenarios—four very bad days.[6] The text of those scenarios follows.

Very Bad Day No. 1: A Nuclear Terrorist Attack
A high-level Russian source under Central Intelligence Agency (CIA) control reveals details of a missing tactical nuclear weapon from the stockpile at a Siberian storage site. The weapon is believed to be headed to a suspected terrorist organization operating in Iraq. Subsequent communications intercepts between Iraqi and Syrian officials and unnamed persons in the United States reveal plans to smuggle a "special" device into the "land of Satan." Overhead reconnaissance satellites detect a suspicious convoy en route from Iraq to Syria. Information sharing among U.S. intelligence organizations is muddled, because the CIA, the National Security Agency (NSA), and the Air Force lack smooth pathways for exchanging data. Moreover, information sharing between the intelligence community and federal law enforcement is obstructed due to the presence of sensitive source materials and legal restrictions associated with domestic collection activities. Western allies are contacted, but the United States refuses to divulge the source of the information. Several Western allies refuse to give the United States' warning any credibility, believing it to be a ruse by the United States to strengthen international resolve with respect to sanctions against Iraq. Given the magnitude of the response required, along with the disruption of normal functioning for many state and local

organizations and entities, the ability of the Federal Emergency Management Agency (FEMA) to mobilize resources (both human and basic supplies) is rapidly overwhelmed. The president orders the Department of Defense (DOD) to provide military support to civil authorities in accord with the Federal Response Plan, but defense medical assistance and other disaster relief measures are not forthcoming due to transportation blockages and an inability to sustain operations in a radiological environment.

Very Bad Day No. 2: A Radiological Terrorist Attack
Building on the first very bad day, a Russian organized crime syndicate steals radioactive isotopes from various unprotected nuclear and medical research laboratories in Russia. The material is sold to a radical Serbian group opposed to the United States' policy in the Balkans. The isotopes as well as plastique are smuggled into Canada and, from there, into the United States through an unprotected border crossing. Once in the United States, the smuggler heads for Rich Stadium in Buffalo. Sitting among a crowd of 80,000, he detonates the weapon, creating a small explosion but spreading radiological material throughout the stadium.

Buffalo firefighters race to the site but cannot enter due to fleeing fans. Buffalo riot police, however, are subsequently able to enter the stadium and restore order. Without radiation detectors, the police are exposed to radiological fallout. Firefighters and hazardous materials (HAZMAT) teams, now able to access the premises, detect the radiation and set up decontamination equipment, but the equipment can decontaminate only 500 people per hour. A near-riot situation ensues. Real and sympathetic victims, suffering from radiation exposure and psychosomatic or stress-related symptoms, respectively, quickly overrun area hospitals. Population dislocation also results—on both sides of the border—as people flee what they think is a contaminated area.

Very Bad Day No. 3: A Chemical Terrorist Attack
A Utah-based vinyl processing plant is shutting down in a matter of weeks and relocating to Mexico. An enraged employee decides to "take action" against the federal government that had supported the North American Free Trade Agreement. What better symbol of government could there be than the IRS, the worker thinks. After stealing a 50-gallon drum of chlorine, the disgruntled and disenfranchised employee steals a vehicle and drives to the IRS processing center in Ogden, located just two hours away. Parking the vehicle upwind of the center, the distraught worker remotely detonates the poisonous cargo—selected because of chlorine's high reactivity with human lungs. The ensuing gas cloud engulfs the center, choking scores of victims instantly and incapacitating hundreds more in the community downwind. Police respond first but refuse to enter the disaster zone without personal protective equipment. As a result, a valuable opportunity to collect criminal evidences is missed. Minutes

later, county HAZMAT teams arrive on the scene, but to little avail, as the scale of the incident overwhelms them.

Very Bad Day No. 4: A Biological Terrorist Attack

No signs or symptoms of an attack manifested themselves during the incubation period following the covert release of a biological agent. The first cases of the illness occur among those with the weakest immune systems: children, elderly, AIDS patients, and patients undergoing chemotherapy. These victims visit their primary care physicians with complaints akin to the flu. Primary care physicians, seeing nothing unusual in either the symptoms or the number of complaints, prescribe over-the-counter medicine, and send the initial victims home to rest. As the biological weapons produce person-to-person disease contagion, the victims infect their family and friends.

As cases mount in number and seriousness, and as odd symptoms manifest themselves, physicians begin to contact fellow physicians and local public health departments. Samples are flown to the nearest laboratory and subsequently to the Centers for Disease Control and Prevention (CDC) laboratory in Atlanta for diagnostic tests. The CDC determines the sample to be a genetically altered strain of smallpox.

The time lag between testing the first patients and diagnosing the cause of their illness allows the disease to spread further. Victims, and people believing themselves to be ill, crowd the hospitals. This depletes the supply of beds and equipment. Hoarding of medication by medical staffs across the country increases sharply. Antivirals are flown into the region, but without a distribution mechanism in place, fail to reach the public. The spread of the disease exponentially complicates the efforts of the CDC and public health officials to trace the origin of the disease. And the use of experimental antiviral agents introduce a host of complicated and novel issues—such as how to obtain informed consent (for use) from recipients and how to administer the agent to large numbers (particularly intravenously).

Containment of the epidemic is the top priority. Yet, the public health and health care communities are unable to work together. The antiquated communications facilities of the public health officials break down under the strain. In addition, despite preexisting policies, such as the Federal Response Plan and Presidential Decision Directive 39, relationships "on the ground" between the FBI, the public health community, or the governor, and emergency responders are ad hoc.

Widespread illness in the community results in significant shortages of personnel, thereby disrupting critical services including telecommunications, electric power, and air traffic control. The rapid spread of the disease causes officials to consider containment and community isolation as the first line of defense. Command, control, and communications prove inadequate, and it is not clear who is in charge.

In the end, a quarantine is instituted, but it is too late. Public health, law enforcement, and emergency response personnel are ill prepared to implement such an untested measure. Public health officials mishandle the announcement of the quarantine, sparking panic in outlying communities and causing thousands to flee. Pressured by their own fearful populations, governors of the surrounding states deploy the National Guard to prevent citizens from the infected state from entering. Unable to enter surrounding states, while unwilling to return to their homes, thousands of citizens become refugees. Civil order collapses.[7]

While focusing on the nuclear, radiological, biological, and chemical threats, the authors of the CSIS report also observed, "conventional explosives could, of course, produce results similar in magnitude to those from a CRBN attack. Consider for example, what would have happened if the bombing of the World Trade Center [in 1993] had collapsed one tower onto the other. In that scenario, 50,000 people could have been killed."[8]

Chemical and Biological Weapons

Poison gas was first used on a wide scale in World War I. German troops deployed chlorine gas against the Allies in 1915 at the battle of Ypres, causing 5,000 deaths. The Allies in turn used poison gas against Germans in Loos, Belgium, five months later. Poison gas was subsequently used at the battles of Fey-en-Haye, Verdun, and Somme. The total of people killed by chlorine, phosgene, and mustard gas in World War I was estimated to be from 500,000 to 1.2 million. The Germans forged ahead of the Allies in their manufacture of chemical weaponry in World War II, developing both tabun and sarin; fortunately, poison gas was not used. Since World War II, chemical weapons have not been widely used in warfare, a notable exception being the Middle East (Saddam Hussein used poison gas, such as tabun, against Iran and Kurds in northern Iraq). Chemical weapons developed after World War II are far more deadly than their predecessors are. Sarin, GB, and VX, for example, can cause instantaneous death. Many chemical substances have legitimate uses and could be easily obtained by terrorists. Quantities of various chemicals such as insecticides, herbicides, rodenticides, and cleaning agents are stored and transported in vast quantities by commercial enterprises and the military and go easily unaccounted for when stolen. Terrorists can also produce their own chemical weapons from legal and easily acquired substances such as isopropyl alcohol. Experts also agree that the technical requirements to produce chemical weapons are not that great (less than that required to produce biological weapons), with knowledge needed only somewhere on the level of a "conscientious graduate student." The real difficulty in waging chemical terrorism lies not with acquisition and manufacture, but with the dissemination of the agent. Wind direction and air temperature affect vapors; nerve gases hydrolyze in water and therefore cannot be used to poison reservoirs, while dispersal in aerosols results in a loss of toxicity. Attempts to use chemical agents by terrorists have occurred in several countries, but the results have been "amateurish" and largely unsuccessful (a notable exception being the "Supreme Truth" cult in the 1995 Tokyo subway attack, where a release of sarin gas killed a dozen people).[9]

Biological warfare dates back much farther than the use of chemical weapons. More than two thousand years ago, Scythian archers dipped their arrows in feces and rotting corpses to increase the deadliness of their weapons. Some believe that Tatars, who catapulted decaying corpses into the besieged city of Caffa, began the black plague that wiped out one-third of Europe in the fourteenth century. During the French and Indian War, British soldiers gave Native Americans blankets sown with smallpox. While all major powers prepared for biological warfare during and after World War I, only Japan actually carried out its plans. She dropped plague-infested fleas and grain over Chinese cities in 1937 and developed a special biological warfare unit called 731 that produced plague, smallpox, typhus, and gas gangrene. The Japanese tested these agents on Chinese prisoners of war and civilians, killing about ten thousand. Although there is some dispute over whether biological agents have been used since World War II, there is no doubt that all of the major powers and several smaller countries have developed and stockpiled these weapons. Up to fifteen countries in the Middle East and Asia have biological weapons and missiles capable of delivering deadly germ payloads. The U.S. State Department has said that the Soviets used mycotoxins called "yellow rain" against enemy forces in Laos, Kampuchea, and Afghanistan, killing thousands. In 1993, then U.S. Chief of Staff Colin Powell said, "the one thing that frightens me to death, perhaps even more so than tactical nuclear weapons, and the one we have the least capability against, is biological weapons." In the meeting when the first President Bush sent American forces to war against Iraq in 1991, officials said that the president had only two last-minute concerns: a last-minute diplomatic move by France and the threat from biological weapons.[10]

A 1972 study concluded that an anthrax-spore aerosol attack on New York City could result in 600,000 deaths, while a pound or two of *Salmonella typhi* or *Clostridium botulinum* in a water reservoir would be just as effective as ten tons of potassium cyanide. Toxicity of biological agents varies, with tularemia and anthrax being the most deadly: They have a downwind range of 20 kilometers and a potential kill of 30,000 to 95,000. Biological weapons are generally more deadly than chemical weapons (the *C. botulinum* toxin is a thousand times more deadly than sarin) and are also relatively easy to manufacture, inexpensive, and difficult to detect once deployed. Acquisition of seed cultures is simple: They can be stolen from labs, bought on the black market, and commissioned by mail order. Specimen cultures can be purchased from commercial firms for a few dollars. Experts disagree on the technical skills required to produce a biological weapon, some arguing that a second year biology student could grow lethal agents in a kitchen laboratory, while others contend that a team of graduate-level scientists and access to a bacteriological lab would be necessary. Like chemical agents, the real difficulty in engineering a biological terrorist attack is deployment: Changes in temperature and wind direction affect germs, they have a limited life span, and the means of delivery are usually complicated (the detonation of a conventional bomb would kill most germs). Although there have been a few successful small-scale attacks (the Rajneesh religious cult infected 750 people with salmonella through a salad bar in Oregon), there have been to date no large-scale biological attacks by terrorists. Perhaps the greatest deterrent to attack by terrorists with either biological or chemical weapons is the political fallout from such an attack. Chemical and biological weapons are also unpredictable and would likely kill friend and foe alike. Still, terrorist groups like al-Qaeda, who wish to kill as many Westerners as possible (they do not seek to influence an audience like many political terrorist groups), or Aum Shinrikyo, who have as their goal the elimination of the entire human race, would not be deterred by the threat of adverse public reaction.[11]

The Nuclear Threat

Transnational criminals are prominently involved in the smuggling of weapons-grade nuclear substances and other potentially harmful radiological materials. Between 1991 and 1995 alone, approximately 440 incidents were documented in which attempts were made to smuggle nuclear materials into Germany, which is considered to be the "hub of nuclear terrorism."[12] Russian mafiya gangs, including Chechens, Ukrainians, Georgians, and one of the more powerful groups, the Dolgopruadnanskaya, are prominent in the theft of nuclear materials. Smugglers also include former Red Army soldiers, former KGB agents, ex-officers of the Stasi (the East German secret service), German-based Russian mafiya gangs, the Italian Mafia, South African groups, and the Serbian mafia, who transport or attempt to transport nuclear materials out of the former Soviet Republics through Eastern Europe, into Germany, and on to clients in Libya, Iraq, Iran, Algeria, and Pakistan. Fortunately, most of the reported thefts consist of low-grade uranium, cesium-137, strontium-90, and cobalt-60—materials that are environmentally hazardous but cannot be used to make nuclear bombs.[13] Nevertheless, terrorists can use radioactive substances such as these quite effectively. Since the September 11, 2001, terrorist attacks, authorities have intercepted terrorist plans that involved the explosion of a so-called "dirty bomb," a conventional explosive packed with radiological materials. While the devastation of such an attack would not be as great as a nuclear explosion, the spread of radioactive materials over a several blocks of a dense metropolitan region could kill and injury thousands.[14] Rensselaer Lee has noted the seriousness of the problem, observing that supply chains and transportation mechanisms are well established in the former Soviet Republics and that the theft of nuclear materials from Russian submarine bases is a growing concern.[15]

In 1994, 1,300 pounds of uranium originating in Kazakhstan that was intended for Saddam Hussein was successfully intercepted and is now stored in Tennessee.[16] Paul N. Woessner compiled a chronology of radioactive and nuclear smuggling incidents from July 1991 to June 1997, an effort that documented 345 separate incidents.[17]

THE THREAT FROM RADICAL ISLAM

While domestic terrorism in the United States has maintained a consistent presence, and right-wing militias and ecoterrorists have received considerable press, the most significant threat to the United States from terrorists is foreign in origin and driven by radical Islam.

Wahhabism emerged with the pretense of reforming Islam in the central area of Arabia in the eighteenth century. It is in reality an extreme, puritanical, and violent terrorist movement founded by Ibn Abd al-Wahhab, who founded an alliance with the house of Saud. The Wahhabi-Saudi axis, where the descendants of al-Wahhab maintain religious authority and the descendants of al-Saud hold political power, continues to the present day. At the outset, Wahhabism declared traditional Muslims to be unbelievers, subject to robbery, murder, and sexual exploitation. The Wahhabists and neo-Wahhabists—principally the Egyptian Muslim Brotherhood and the Pakistani Islamists—are the primary sources of Islamic terrorism in the world. Moreover, Wahhabism is completely subsidized by the Saudi regime and its oil revenue. Wahhabism is official in Saudi Arabia and influential in Kuwait, Yemen, the United Arab Emirates, and Qatar. The Hamas terrorist group in Israel represents a pure form of Wahhabism. Wahhabi aggression was defeated in Algeria and Tajikistan (as well as Afghanistan with the U.S.-led overthrow of the Taliban regime), but is present in Chechnya, Kashmir, East Africa (including the Khartoum regime in Sudan), the Philippines, and Indonesia.

Wahhabism is a serious problem within the United States, for it is the only country outside of Saudi Arabia where the Islamic establishment is under Wahhabi control. Eighty percent of American mosques are Wahhabi-influenced, and official Muslim organizations such as the Council on American Islamic Relations, the Islamic Society of North America, the American Muslim Council, and the Muslim Students Association in the United States are all fronts for Wahhabism. This violent and radicalized form of Islam is bred in the nation's prisons and on some college campuses.[18]

Principal Islamic Terrorist Groups That Pose a Threat to the United States

Hamas was formed in 1987 as an offshoot of the Egyptian-based Muslim brotherhood. The group's goal is the expulsion of all Jews from Israel and the creation of an Islamic Palestinian state ruled by strict theocratic law known as shari'a. Since the latest renewal of violence in Israel beginning in the fall of 2000, Hamas has been responsible for at least twenty-seven suicide bombings causing scores of casualties. Recruits for such efforts could be large, as the group numbers its supporters in the tens of thousands. The group is truly transnational in nature, since the bulk of Hamas's funding comes from outside Israel. Palestinian expatriates and other sources in Saudi Arabia and other Gulf States, especially Iran, provide significant financial support. Much of the money is funneled through Islamic charitable organizations engaged in overt charitable work, making interception of assets complicated. In December 2001, the Bush administration seized the Holy Land Foundation, the largest Muslim charity in the United States, for allegedly funding Hamas.[19]

The Abu Sayyaf group (ASG) was founded in 1991. Its name means "Bearer of the Sword." Abu Sayyaf was begun under the leadership of Abduragak Abubakar Janjalani, who studied in Libya and Saudi Arabia before training as a mujaheddin to fight the Soviets in Afghanistan. U.S. intelligence officials believe it was here that Janjalani first met Usama bin Laden. Philippine police killed Janjalani in December 1998, and his younger brother and Ghalib Andang replaced him as the nominal leaders of the group. In October 1997, the U.S. State Department designated ASG as one of the top thirty foreign terrorist organizations in the world. The ASG claims to be fighting for an independent Muslim homeland in the southern Philippines. Authorities believe the group is funded by al-Qaeda as a part of its strategy to turn Southeast Asia into a Pan-Islamic region. ASG activities involve primarily kidnappings for ransom. On May 27, 2001, ASG kidnapped twenty people, including three Americans. The terrorists beheaded one of the Americans, Guillermo Sobero, and held a Christian missionary couple until June 2002. At that time, American hostage Martin Burnham was killed, but his wife was rescued after being held for over eleven months. Earlier in June 2002, the Bush administration deployed 1,200 advisors to help train Philippine soldiers in their fight against ASG. The training mission ended on July 31, 2002, but 300 U.S. troops remained to help with infrastructure projects. In addition to the higher profile international kidnappings, the Abu Sayyaf regularly terrorize local populations. More than 300 Filipino soldiers have died in the fight to eliminate ASG.[20]

Usama bin Laden established al-Qaeda in the late 1980s. He helped to finance, recruit, transport, and train Sunni Islamic extremists for the Afghan resistance against the Soviet invasion in 1980. The goal of the group is to create a Pan-Islamic Caliphate throughout the world by collaborating with other Islamic terrorist organizations to overthrow non-Islamic regimes. The group issued a statement in 1998 declaring that it was the duty of all Muslims to kill U.S. citizens, civilian and military. In June 2001, al-Qaeda merged with Egyptian Islamic Jihad (Al-Jihad). The Egyptian Islamic Jihad has operatives in Europe, Yemen, Pakistan, Lebanon, and Afghanistan. The al-Qaeda network is part of an intricate web of alliances with Sunni extremists worldwide, including North Africans, radical Palestinians, Pakistanis, and Central Asians. It finances and provides training and logistics to Islamic militants in Afghanistan, Algeria, Bosnia, Chechnya, Eritrea, Iraq, Kosovo, the Philippines, Somalia, Tajikistan, Yemen, and Kosovo, and has been linked to conflicts and attacks in Africa, Asia, Europe, the former Soviet Republics, the Middle East, and North and South America. Terrorist groups affiliated with al-Qaeda are responsible for the August 1998 attacks against the U.S. embassies in Kenya and Tanzania, the October 2000 attack against the USS *Cole* in Aden, Yemen, and the catastrophic attacks on the Pentagon and the World Trade Center in September 2001. Although law enforcement operations (including the freezing of assets used to fund terrorists) and the U.S. war in Afghanistan that toppled the Taliban helped to disperse and eliminate al-Qaeda operatives, as of mid-2003, the threat from this group was still considered significant.[21]

Hezbollah, meaning "Party of God," formed in 1982 in response to the Israeli invasion of Lebanon. A Lebanon-based Shi'a group, it is inspired by the Iranian Revolution and the teachings of the Ayatollah Khomeini. Closely allied with and often directed by the Iranian state, Hezbollah has also been a tactical ally in helping Syria to advance its political objectives in the Middle East. The group also has a stated objective of eliminating the state of Israel. Hezbollah has successfully attacked the United States, including the suicide truck bombings of the U.S. Embassy and a U.S. Marine barracks in Beirut in April and October 1983, where hundreds of Marines were killed. The group has also kidnapped and held hostage U.S. citizens and other Westerners in Lebanon, and is responsible for the hijacking of TWA Flight 847 in 1985 in which a U.S. navy diver was murdered. Hezbollah has several hundred operatives and thousands of supporters worldwide, with active cells in Europe, Africa, South America, North America, and Asia. Iran provides money, training, weapons, explosives and political, diplomatic, and organization aid, while the state of Syria provides diplomatic, political, and logistical support.[22]

CYBERTERRORISM

The integration of information systems and the dependence of banking, defense, air traffic control, and other vital systems on computer networks have created new national security concerns. By 1996, the U.S. National Security Strategy stated that threat of information warfare and the acts of so-called cyberterrorists posed a significant national security threat.[23] The Presidential Commission on Critical Infrastructure Protection (PCCIP) found in 1997 that the United States was highly vulnerable to cyberattacks. U.S. adversaries could conduct strategic attacks on information infrastructures using mechanical, electromagnetic, and digital means. Mechanical attacks include activities such as the bombing of command and control systems and the cutting of fiber-optic cables, while the direction of electromagnetic pulses at specific targets could disrupt or destroy communication and information systems.[24]

Digital intrusion into U.S. government computer systems has been well documented. In the late 1980s, a group of German teenagers in the employ of the KGB broke into more than forty sensitive DOD, Department of Energy, and NASA computer systems, while during the Gulf War of the early 1990s, hackers from the Netherlands penetrated thirty-four DOD systems, modifying and storing military data on systems at major U.S. universities. In early 1994, hackers used a "password sniffer" to access computer networks at Griffis Air Force Base in New York, which they used as a launching point for intrusions into NASA's Goddard Space Flight Center in Maryland, NATO headquarters in Brussels, and the Korean Nuclear Research Center in Seoul. In 1995 and 1996, an Argentinean intruder accessed the Harvard University network to access other networks at the Naval Research Laboratory and other DOD, NASA, and Los Alamos National Laboratory computers. The systems accessed contained highly sensitive information on radar technology, aircraft design, and satellite command and control systems. In February 1998, two teenagers in California under the guidance of an eighteen-year-old Israeli mentor hacked into numerous DOD military computer networks using foreign computer systems, including one in the United Arab Emirates. The DOD characterized the intrusions as the "most organized and systematic attack" on U.S. defense networks discovered at that time. A test in 1994 of DOD computers using well-known digital attack techniques accessed 88 percent of DOD networks, while only 4 percent of systems' operators detected the intrusions.[25]

Of course, governmental agencies other than the DOD are highly susceptible to computer hackers. The Web sites of many U.S. government agencies have been broken into and changed, including the Department of Justice and the CIA. Private telephone network and Internet service companies have been targeted as well: Hackers have disrupted 911 emergency notification systems by misdirecting calls. Intercepts of the digital signatures of cellular phones create "clones" used to assign costs to unsuspecting victims, a practice also highly useful for communications among criminals. In a process referred to as "phreaking," hackers use physical and digital techniques to access the networks of AT&T, MCI, and other phone companies in order to make free calls. In 1997, another teenage hacker disabled Bell Atlantic telephone communication switches in the northeastern United States and shut down the Worcester, Massachusetts, airport for several hours. America Online, the nation's largest Internet Service Provider (ISP), is continually the target of hacker attacks. In December 1994, a group calling itself the INTERNET Liberation Front was charged with stealing phone data, perpetrating Internet attacks for money, and developing sophisticated attack tools. The group, with members from at least eight different countries, targeted numerous ISPs, including some that support the U.S. government.[26]

Cyberattackers have also targeted commercial users of information infrastructures, most notably banking and financial institutions. By 1999, an FBI survey found that 62 percent of banking respondents reported unauthorized use of their computer systems within the last twelve months, and an additional 21 percent did not know if their systems had been illegally accessed. A Russian hacker siphoned off $12 million in funds electronically in 1995. In 1991, a hacker stole an automaker's future car designs valued at $500 million, and in 1998, hackers exploited a bug in Microsoft's Windows NT operating system, causing thousands of computers at NASA and major universities to crash. A 1997 FBI survey found that 40 percent of information security managers at Fortune 500 companies reported that their companies had suffered computer break-ins within the previous year.[27]

Another well-publicized form of cyberattack is the use of computer viruses, software designed to make copies of itself as it spreads from computer to computer, creating operational problems and erasing entire hard drives. In 1987, there were only six known viruses; by 1997, there were over 10,000. Throughout 1999 and 2000, a series of virulent outbreaks like "Melissa" and "I Love You" disrupted government, commercial, and other private information systems worldwide. Other malicious software such as "logic bombs," "time bombs," "Trojan horse" programs, and "trapdoors" take effect only when certain conditions are met, such as the arrival of a certain date or the performance of certain key strokes. Hackers often use a method called salami slicing to siphon off huge amounts of cash from separate accounts a few pennies (or fractions of pennies) at a time. Company and agency insiders are well placed to cause significant disruptions as well as the siphoning of funds. For example, a single officer of a Wells Fargo Bank caused $21.3 million in losses due to computer fraud; the National Bonded Insurance Company sustained a $141,000 loss from a "Trojan horse" that diverted money orders at the rate of $1,000 a day; the USPA and IRA brokerage and insurance firm lost 168,000 sales commission records due to a "logic bomb" that erased portions of the main computer's memory; a logic bomb deleted the Omega Engineering Corporation's design and production programs, resulting in damages of $10 million. Information infrastructures can also be damaged by the purposeful insertion of flawed software at any point throughout the process of research, development, manufacturing, and distribution.[28]

Digital intrusion for the purposes of pirating intellectual property and economic state-sponsored espionage has also been detected. Using automated tools, a hacker can scan a network for vulnerabilities, choose a tool that creates access, gain control, insert enabling software, and depart within minutes without notice. The insertion of a "back door" allows the hacker to access the system at his leisure. Graphical user interfaces and programs such as "Rootkit" and "Watcher T" have facilitated the ease and speed of digital attacks. Rootkit is a software command language that, when run on a UNIX computer permits complete access and control of the machine's data and network interfaces. Watcher T is a high-technology Artificial Intelligence engine designed to look for thousands of vulnerabilities in all computers and networks, including PCs, UNIX (client/server), and mainframes.[29]

TERRORIST FINANCING

Terrorists finance their activities through criminal activities, such as drug trafficking, cigarette smuggling, robbery, kidnapping, extortion, and currency counterfeiting, yet the largest portion of funds that finance terrorist organizations are derived from contributors. These contributors include nongovernmental organizations and otherwise legitimate commercial entities. Charitable donations are often commingled with other funds and then siphoned or diverted to groups that support terrorism. Transactions that finance terrorism are typically small enough to avoid notification requirements and are often camouflaged as legitimate business, social, or charitable activity, while the movement of funds is accomplished by the usual money laundering methods, including informal, difficult to monitor banking systems like the hawala, hundi, fei ch'ien, phoe kuan, ch'iao hui, and nging sing kek. The misuse of hawala and other alternative remittance systems by terrorist organizations has been well documented. On November 7, 2001, the U.S. government blocked the assets of Al Barakaat, a financial and telecommunications conglomerate with operations in forty countries around the world. United States authorities seized records and closed Al Barakaat offices in four states, and on the same day, international officials closed down a hybrid hawala operation known as Al-Barakaat—Al-Barakaat had been used to move money through Dubai into Somalia and other countries.[30]

CHAPTER 6

Responding to Transnational Organized Crime

This chapter will provide an overview of recent legislative, judicial, administrative, and law enforcement efforts to combat the rapid spread of transnational crimes. Because the United States did not even formally recognize transnational crime as a national security threat until the mid-1990s, it is fair to say that the response has been tardy and certainly limited in terms of effect. The global dimensions of the problem, its diffuse and expansive nature, the widespread corruption of public officials, and the challenges of international cooperation hinder attempts to strike at transnational criminal networks. Increasing global demand for drugs and other black market commodities drive the transnational crime engine, while religious zealotry, ethnic rivalries, and ideological radicals fuel international terrorism and its catastrophic progeny. Moreover, while strong legislation and technological innovation give government and private sector personnel tools to fight criminals, the tools themselves give rise to serious questions regarding privacy rights and the scope of government power.

The chapter will begin with an examination of the legislative foundations of organized crime control: the Omnibus Crime Control and Safe Streets Act of 1968, the Racketeer Influenced and Corrupt Organizations Act (RICO), and laws that provide for the seizure or forfeiture of assets derived from criminal activity. Next we will look at initiatives to combat drug trafficking and money laundering. Due to the primacy and timeliness of the topics, an in-depth discussion of the response to the September 11 terrorist attacks will be provided, including a detailed analysis of the USA Patriot Act, the Homeland Security Act, and other measures related to border security, the detection and surveillance of transnational criminals, and efforts to block the financing of terrorist activities. Finally, the chapter will conclude with a look at international dimensions of transnational crime control, including an examination of the United Nations' Palermo Convention, the role of Interpol, and the possibilities for the International Criminal Court.

ELECTRONIC SURVEILLANCE, RICO, AND ASSET FORFEITURE

Perhaps the most significant U.S. law enacted to fight organized crime was Title III of the Omnibus Crime Control and Safe Streets Act of 1968. This piece of legislation provided for judicially approved electronic surveillance by federal, state, and local law enforcement officials (intercepted conversations have been a key component of nearly every major organized crime prosecution in the latter half of the twentieth century). Amendments in 1986 provided for roving surveillance, additionally arming law enforcement with the legal authority to monitor criminal or potentially criminal activities. A part of the Organized Crime Control Act of 1970, the Racketeer Influenced and Corrupt Organizations Act (RICO) is based on the legal concept that participation in the affairs of a criminal enterprise is a crime in itself. In addition to punishing underlying predicate acts, such as gambling, narcotics trafficking, and extortion, RICO made it a crime to participate in or conduct the affairs of an enterprise through a pattern of racketeering activity. Now prosecutors could try multiple criminal defendants as a group and attack *patterns* of criminal activity, meting out severe criminal penalties as well as civil measures that allowed the government to obtain injunctions to prevent racketeers from controlling labor unions and other legitimate enterprises. Along with the Continuing Criminal Enterprise provisions of the Comprehensive Drug Abuse Prevention and Control Act of 1970, RICO revived the practice of asset forfeiture, allowing the government to seize property derived from or used in the commission of crimes. Armed with the leverage of hefty prison sentences (in the case *U.S. v. Salerno*, Cosa Nostra bosses were sentenced to one hundred years), prosecutors placed organized criminals into the Witness Protection Program in exchange for useful testimony—another powerful tool used in major organized crime prosecutions. Although many law enforcement efforts against organized crime in America have been largely domestic prosecutions, some have taken on international dimensions. A notable example is *U.S. v. Badalementi*, commonly referred to as the "Pizza Connection" case. A cooperative effort among American, Italian, Swiss, Brazilian, and Spanish law enforcement agencies disrupted a network of

American Cosa Nostra and Sicilian Mafia groups who used American pizza shops as fronts for a $1.6 billion heroin trafficking enterprise. In fact, under RICO, the United States has been successful at extending its laws extraterritorially, especially in drug and money laundering cases. Moreover, the significant RICO penalties are just as applicable, and have in fact been broadly applied, to a range of racketeers that include not only crime bosses, but also the lawyers, accountants, and investment bankers who play such a major role in the organization of crime.[1]

Civil forfeiture is a legal proceeding against property believed to be used in criminal activity. Civil forfeiture was first authorized by the first Congress of the United States and does not require a criminal conviction for property to be seized by the government. Criminal forfeiture was first authorized in 1970 with the enactment of the RICO and Continuing Criminal Enterprise statutes as part of the criminal action taken against persons convicted of crimes related to drug trafficking, money laundering, and racketeering. Unlike civil forfeiture, a conviction is required before the government can seize property. At present, forfeiture laws have been expanded to include a wide variety of crimes, from soliciting prostitution to playing cards for money. The range of property seized is great and includes currency, other financial instruments, real property, vehicles, vessels, and aircraft. The 1984 Federal Comprehensive Forfeiture Act increased the government's ability to confiscate the assets of *suspected* drug dealers under federal law. In civil forfeiture cases, the quantum of proof required to seize assets is only a preponderance of the evidence—a lower standard than in criminal cases.[2]

Since 1988, property or assets involved in specific illegal transactions can be forfeited and even used to pay for one's own prosecution. Law enforcement agencies embraced the new forfeiture laws enthusiastically and used the prospect of seized funds to induce informants and to encourage foreign governments to assist in money laundering investigations. The UN Convention against Illicit Traffic in Narcotic Drugs and Psychotropic Substances (the Vienna Convention) is perhaps the most important development in international forfeiture cooperation. Article V of the Vienna Convention details the obligations of parties seeking forfeiture of drug trafficking or money laundering proceeds, and required signatory countries to enact laws with domestic and international implications. In 1992, the U.S. Congress enacted a statute (28 U.S.C. section 1355(b)(2)) vesting U.S. district courts with extraterritorial jurisdiction over assets located abroad that are subject to civil forfeiture while furthering the United States' ability to lend assistance to other nations in international forfeiture cases. Statute 18 U.S.C. section 981 permits the use of foreign forfeiture orders and convictions to support a civil forfeiture action against drug proceeds found in the United States. It has also been U.S. policy to share seized assets with countries that made possible or facilitated the forfeiture of assets under U.S. law. Between 1989 and 1999, the U.S. Department of Justice transferred more than $65 million of seized assets to twenty-one different countries. By July 2000, a total of $169 million had been transferred to twenty-six different countries. Authorities have observed that such asset sharing substantially enhances international cooperation in forfeiture cases.

In the years 1985 to 1994, the Department of Justice won forfeiture of more than $3.8 billion in addition to unsold properties appraised at $277.7 million. While one federal appellate court has ruled that the warrantless seizure of wire transfers does not violate the Fourth Amendment so long as probable cause exists that a crime was committed, aggressive forfeiture of assets prior to conviction has come under increasing criticism on constitutional grounds. In the case *U.S. v. $405,089.23*, the Ninth Circuit ruled that civil forfeiture following a criminal conviction constituted double jeopardy, a violation of the Sixth Amendment. The Civil Asset Forfeiture Reform Act of 2000 made it slightly more difficult for the U.S. government to seize assets. It now must establish probable cause that the seized property was derived or involved in criminal activity. Other levels of proof required include a preponderance of the evidence to win civil forfeiture and proof beyond a reasonable doubt to win criminal forfeiture.[3]

RECENT INITIATIVES IN THE "WAR ON DRUGS"

The U.S. National Drug Control Strategy, in addition to its education and treatment components, is focused on disrupting illegal drug markets. As such, the governmental response is to view the drug trade as a business enterprise, with the goal of increasing the costs of doing business. A major player in this effort is the Department of Justice's Organized Crime Drug Enforcement Task Force (OCDETF) program, created in 1982 with the goal of dismantling major drug trafficking organizations and their money laundering operations. Recently, the OCDETF and its nine member organizations have refocused their efforts on financial and multijurisdictional investigations aimed at the most significant drug trafficking groups. For fiscal year 2004, the Bush administration proposed a $72 million increase for the OCDETF program, with a large chunk of the overall appropriation going to the IRS's Criminal Investigative Division charged with combating money laundering. Both the High Intensity Drug Trafficking Areas (HIDTA) program and the Consolidated Priority Organization Target (CPOT) list strive to engineer unity of effort among law enforcement agencies, with a concentration of resources directed at the most significant drug traffickers.

The International Emergency Economic Powers Act and Executive Order 12978 (dated October 21, 1995) directed the Secretary of the Treasury and the Attorney General to identify businesses and people used as fronts for Colombian narcotics traffickers, to bar U.S. persons from having property or commercial transactions with these so-called "specially designated narcotics traffickers" (SDNTs), and to block their assets in the United States or assets held in U.S. banks overseas. By December 1997, forty-one SDNT companies had been liquidated, while Colombian banks had closed 200 accounts affecting nearly one hundred SDNTs.

The United States also works with the UN Drug Control Program (UNDCP) and seeks to advance the goals of the 1988 UN Drug Convention (the Vienna Convention). Through the UNDCP, recent White House administrations have helped to finance and implement counternarcotics programs in Burma and Afghanistan, leverage Western European support for international antidrug efforts, establish drug control institutions in former Soviet satellite countries and Eastern Europe, and provide training and technical assistance to countries implementing chemical control programs. Through the Dublin group, which meets annually, the Department of State disseminates information to other governments concerning U.S. counternarcotics activities.[4]

The success of the U.S. war on drugs and appropriate public policies are still hotly debated. The official U.S. government position is that so-called "experts" are wrong. Success in severely limiting drug consumption is possible through prohibition and a combination of education, treatment, and law enforcement measures. For example, the 2002 National Drug Control Strategy from the Bush White House observed that in 2001, the U.S. government and partner nations interdicted about 28 percent of the cocaine shipped into the United States—within reach of the 35 percent to 50 percent rate required to precipitate a major disruption in the cocaine market.[5] Critics of prohibition point to continued high levels of illicit drug consumption, corruption, and organized crime driven by the global black market, the hopelessly porous U.S. borders, and the erosion of civil liberties. It is safe to conclude that the debate will continue, as will the war on drugs.

COMBATING MONEY LAUNDERING

Among all transnational crimes, the outlook on fighting money laundering is especially grim. Methods and characteristics of money laundering are apparently limited only by the imagination of the given criminal and differ based on the type of crime it is associated with, making it even more difficult for law enforcers to identify and recognize patterns. For example, with real estate fraud, developers acquire large loans, wire the money to bank accounts outside the United States, and then declare bankruptcy. With terrorism and the illegal trade in arms and nuclear materials, methods can vary because criminals typically intend to conceal the destination as well as the origin of funds.

Despite the ease with which funds now flow across international borders, law enforcement still believes that the best hope is to attack money laundering at the placement stage—that point where the money launderer first seeks to enter the ill-gained funds into the financial system. Because of this focus, banks and other depository institutions remain the first line of defense. In fact, with a few exceptions, the U.S. government has succeeded in stopping launderers from gaining direct access to U.S. banks. As a result, money launderers now look increasingly to international mechanisms and nonbank money transmitters. Major factors that now confound law enforcement include:

- the full-scale automation of wire transfer services with increased on-line access and less human intervention or monitoring;
- the exponential growth of international and multinational business transactions;
- the interdependence of financial institutions and clearing mechanisms globally;
- the increase in correspondent relationships between U.S. and foreign banks, and specialized bank accounts that cater to foreign clients;
- the development of money management services, foreign exchange trading, swaps and derivative trading, and other legitimate financial services that provide cover for money launderers;
- immigration patterns that encourage the proliferation of nonbank money transmitters;
- new trends in banking, such as direct-access banking and cybercurrency;
- the willingness and ability of criminals to shift rapidly among money laundering techniques;
- and the use of underground/informal banking systems, such as the chit system and the hawala.

United States' law enforcers often have difficulty in determining the location of funds due to offshore banks with representative offices in other foreign countries. Knowing which jurisdiction to focus forfeiture efforts on is problematic and is exacerbated by weak forfeiture laws in foreign jurisdictions and the incompatibility of those laws with U.S. statutes. Limited cooperation from foreign countries and legal issues associated with jurisdiction and venue are formidable obstacles.[6]

"Know-your-customer" policies at banks and cash reporting requirements have not succeeded in blocking access of money launderers to bank accounts and wire transfers services. Moreover, such methods are likely to become even more ineffective for a variety of reasons. The world banking community knows no geographic bounds, is open for business twenty-four hours a day, and is increasingly interconnected as multinational banks extend the scope of their operations through branch and subsidiary networks and through correspondent relationships that span the globe. Phil Williams of the Ridgway Center for International Security Studies has flatly concluded that "the global financial system provides many more opportunities than law enforcement can ever hope to forestall or block."[7]

Money Laundering Legislation

A significant legislative attempt in the United States to thwart tax evasion and money laundering was the Currency and Foreign Transactions Reporting Act, more commonly referred to as the Bank Secrecy Act (BSA) of 1970. The intent of the act was to create an audit trail that would allow police to track large cash transactions. Although money laundering was not specifically prohibited, the act required that banks file a Currency Transaction Report (CTR) for every cash transaction over $10,000. Persons importing or exporting more than $10,000 into or out of the United States were required to file an International Transportation of Currency or Monetary Instruments Report (CMIR). Additionally, U.S. citizens or residents were required to file a Foreign Bank and Financial Accounts Report (FBAR) if they held a foreign bank account. Additional requirements were imposed in 1984 when businesses other than financial institutions (such as auto dealers) were ordered to report cash transactions over $10,000. Money laundering itself was not criminalized until passage of the Money Laundering Control Act of 1986, which mandated penalties of up to twenty years and fines up to $500,000 for each count. The 1986 law also outlawed "smurfing," the practice of making numerous transactions just under the $10,000 reporting trigger. The Anti-Drug Abuse Act of 1988 increased civil and criminal penalties for money laundering and other BSA violations, including the forfeiture of any property and assets related to a money laundering transaction.

The 1988 law also empowered the Department of Treasury to negotiate bilateral international agreements for recording and sharing large transactions of U.S. currency. Additional U.S. legislation to combat money laundering includes:

- *The Depository Institution Money Laundering Amendment Act of 1990* that authorizes the federal government to request the assistance of a foreign bank authority and to accommodate such requests from foreign authorities in money laundering investigations;
- *The Annunzio-Wylie Anti–Money Laundering Act of 1992* that requires financial institutions to have compliance procedures and staff training, with noncompliance resulting in charter revocation or termination of Federal Deposit Insurance;
- *The Money Laundering Suppression Act of 1994*, designed to reduce the number of CTRs 30 percent annually by mandating certain exemptions (the huge volume of CTRs was and is overwhelming for investigators). The 1994 Act also requires federal registration of all nonbank money transmitters, including some 10,000 American Express agents, 14,000 Western Union agents, and all currency exchange houses and *giro* houses (neighborhood money transmitters).[8]
- *The "Patriot Act" (2001)* Title III of this wide-ranging act contains significant provisions for combating money laundering and terrorist financing, including allowing financial institutions to share information, allowing FinCEN greater access to financial institution records, establishing a $5,000 reporting threshold for securities brokers, money services businesses, and casinos, and tightening the regulation of correspondent/ foreign-owned bank accounts in the U.S. financial system.[9]

The Office of Technology Assessment and Artificial Intelligence

In 1994, the Senate Permanent Subcommittee on Investigations asked the Office of Technology Assessment (OTA) to assess the feasibility of using artificial intelligence (AI) computer techniques to monitor international wire transfers and detect laundered money. The OTA concluded that real-time monitoring of wire transfers was not feasible. However, the OTA study also concluded that there are several ways in which information technology may be applied to wire transfer records to combat money laundering. Central to OTA proposals is the screening of wire transfers through knowledge-based systems that automatically make inferences about data or link analyses, which identify relationships among individual accounts, people, and organizations. Knowledge acquisition is another integral component of information technologies that may be used to combat money laundering. For example, cluster analysis of wire transfers could be based on the frequency, dollar amount, and destination of each transfer, allowing for the revelation of groups of transfers with similar origins. Similarly, visualization techniques use color and interactive graphics to explore the relationship among variables, while case-based reasoning and neural network technologies may be used to derive money laundering profiles from data and apply those profiles. However, none of the OTA proposals envisioned an effective money laundering enforcement tool using AI that did not also involve a significant burden for banks, intrusions into the financial privacy of legitimate businesses and law-abiding citizens, complications in international relations and issues related to national sovereignty, and expensive systems development. In fact, any effective transnational money laundering effort would necessarily hinder to some degree the legitimate international flow of capital and raise concerns about the role of the dollar in international payment systems.[10]

FinCEN

The Financial Crimes Enforcement Network (FinCEN) was set up by executive order within the Department of the Treasury in 1990. Its mission has been to support federal, state, and local law enforcers and regulators by providing information and analysis, and to identify targets for investigation of money laundering and other financial crimes. FinCEN staff analyzes intelligence from a broad range of government and commercial sources and uses advanced computer techniques, including AI, to link disparate pieces of data and identify patterns that are indicative of illegal activities. FinCEN's Project Gateway allows state law enforcement officials to access directly the IRS database of Currency Transaction Reports, and the Criminal Referral System (CRS) contains reports that identify bank employees, bank customers, and others who have been the subject of Bank Secrecy Act reports, investigations, or prosecutions. The CRS allows on-line access to five regulatory agencies overseeing financial institutions. FinCEN also provides database retrieval systems to law enforcement, analyses of Federal Reserve Bank data on the shipment of currency between member institutions, threat assessments on potential money laundering activities, and assessments of money laundering by country. In 2002, FinCEN established a highly secure network enabling financial institutions to file Suspicious Activity Reports (SARs) electronically.[11]

The Financial Action Task Force (FATF)

In addition to unilateral efforts, the United States has solicited and stimulated international cooperation in the fight against money laundering. The United Nations Convention Against Illicit Traffic in Narcotics Drugs and Psychotropic Substances (the Vienna Convention) entered into force in December 1990 and criminalized money laundering incident to narcotics trafficking—there are well over one hundred signatory states. Foremost among international organizations combating money laundering is the Financial Action Task Force (FATF), created in 1989 at the International Economic Summit as a mechanism for international cooperation in fighting narcotics-related money laundering. In 1994, the FATF broadened its mission to include non–drug-related money laundering. With twenty-nine member nations, FATF seeks to improve contact between experts and law enforcement, document money laundering techniques, and compile national programs targeting money laundering, expand members' legislation so that prosecutions need not depend on some underlying crime, and encourage the formation of regional money laundering task forces (such as the Caribbean Task Force and the Gulf Cooperation Council). The FATF has made forty recommendations, the most significant of which include requiring member states to criminalize the laundering of the proceeds of serious crimes, enact measures to seize illicit assets, permit banks to report suspicious transactions, prohibit banks from maintaining anonymous accounts, and establish international treaties and pass national legislation that fosters transnational cooperation in the fight against money laundering. The U.S. government estimates that about 130 jurisdictions representing 85 percent of the world's population and 90 to 95 percent of global economic output have made political commitments to implementing the forty recommendations. In addition, the G-7, the International Monetary Fund, and the World Bank have recognized the FATF Forty Recommendations as the international standard in the fight against money laundering, while the UN Convention on Transnational Organized Crime (the Palermo Convention) made specific reference to the FATF recommendations in its provision requiring states to implement measures to control money laundering.

In June 2000, the FATF published a list of fifteen noncooperative countries and territories that quickly resulted in a number of those entities acting to implement FATF standards as well (threats to hinder access to IMF and World Bank loans were made). By 2002, most of the noncooperative countries listed by the FATF had enacted significant money laundering reforms, and only one, Nauru, had made insufficient progress triggering FATF countermeasures. In 2001, the FATF began working toward the evaluation and revision of the original forty recommendations, a process that culminated in a May 2002 Special FATF Plenary in Rome. Final revisions were oriented around issues such as customer identification requirements for financial institutions, identification of beneficial owners, the treatment of corporate vehicles and trusts, and the extension of anti–money laundering requirements beyond financial institutions.[12]

The 2002 National Money Laundering Strategy

In 2001, the Bush administration released its first National Money Laundering Strategy, a plan that stressed successful prosecutions, asset forfeiture, advanced money laundering training courses for federal agents and prosecutors, measurement of progress, and improving cooperation and fostering partnerships among federal, state, local, and foreign law enforcement officials, as well as the private sector. The 2002 National Money Laundering Strategy established six broad goals: (1) to measure the effectiveness of anti–money laundering efforts; (2) to focus law enforcement and regulatory resources on identifying, disrupting, and dismantling terrorist financing networks; (3) to increase the investigation and prosecution of major money laundering organizations and systems; (4) to prevent money laundering through cooperative public-private efforts and necessary regulatory measures; (5) to coordinate law enforcement efforts with state and local governments to fight money laundering throughout the United States; and (6) to strengthen international anti–money laundering regimes. Highlights of the 2002 report included the notation that in 2001, the Bush administration negotiated an international agreement with four governments to coordinate an attack against the Black Market Peso Exchange. Law enforcement agencies of the Departments of Treasury and Justice *seized* over $1 billion in criminal assets, $300 million of which was attributable to money laundering operations, and another $639 million was *forfeited*, of which $241 million was related to money laundering. The report also noted that in 2001, the United States provided over $3.5 million in international anti–money laundering training and technical assistance, especially to problem nations attempting reform.

The Bush White House formulated additional objectives and priorities in the 2002 National Money Laundering Strategy. Initiatives include improving collaborative international efforts to isolate terrorist financing networks and provide information to the United States, focusing on the Internet as a source of "cyberfundraising" for terrorist groups, providing technical assistance to jurisdictions willing and committed to fight terrorist financing networks, urging countries and territories to implement counterterrorism

financing standards (the Asian-Pacific Economic Cooperation [APEC]), the
Manila Framework Group, and the Association of South East Asian Nations
(ASEAN) Regional Forum have all agreed to focus their efforts on combat-
ing terrorism and terrorist financing, and refining the mission of High-Risk
Money Laundering and Related Financial Crime Area (HIFCA) task forces.[13]

The Patriot Act, Money Laundering, and Terrorist Financing

On October 26, 2001, President Bush signed into law the Uniting and
Strengthening America by Providing Appropriate Tools Required to Intercept and Obstruct Terrorist Act (the USA PATRIOT Act). Among its very
broad range of provisions were significant new tools for law enforcers and
financial investigators to combat money laundering and secure the forfeiture
of assets related to terrorism. The Patriot Act:

- requires all financial institutions to have an anti–money laundering program in place by April 2002;
- requires the New York Stock Exchange and the National Association of
  Securities Dealers to adopt anti–money laundering programs for the entities they regulate;
- Section 313 prohibits U.S. financial institutions from providing correspondent banking accounts to foreign shell banks and requires those financial
  institutions to take reasonable steps to ensure that their correspondent
  accounts are not used by their foreign clients to provide services to shell
  banks;
- Section 536 requires brokers-dealers in securities to report suspicious
  transactions under BSA provisions; this rule will now extend to money
  service businesses, casinos, and investment companies, including hedge
  funds and private equity funds.[14]

Another priority of the Patriot Act was to enhance mechanisms for the
international exchange of financial intelligence through the support and expansion of membership in the Egmont Group of Financial Intelligence Units
(FIUs). In 2001, FinCEN coordinated 435 investigative intelligence exchanges with 67 foreign jurisdictions, and by July 2002 connected seven new
FIUs to the Egmont Secure Network. In another international development,
the G-7 countries and Mexico established international standards for electronic customs reporting. By using bill of lading numbers, invoice numbers,
or unique consignment reference numbers as standard transaction identifi-

ers, authorities in different nations can quickly identify discrepancies in trade data (utilization of false bills of lading is a common money laundering technique).

After the al-Qaeda terrorist attack on the United States on September 11, 2001, the FATF convened a plenary meeting in Washington, D.C., and adopted eight special recommendations regarding terrorist financing:

- ratification and implementation of UN instruments, including the 1999 United Nations International Convention for the Suppression of the Financing of Terrorism and UN resolutions regarding the suppression of terrorist acts, particularly Security Council Resolution 1373;
- criminalizing the financing of terrorism and associated money laundering—countries should be sure to list acts of terrorism as money laundering predicates;
- freezing and confiscating terrorist assets;
- reporting suspicious transactions related to terrorism—a recommended legal requirement for businesses or entities subject to anti–money laundering obligations;
- ensuring that countries afford one another, by treaty or other arrangement, mutual legal assistance and information exchange in connection with criminal, civil forfeiture, and administrative investigations relating to the financing of terrorism;
- ensuring that persons or legal entities that provide a service for the transmission of money or value, including transmission through an informal or value transfer system, should be licensed or registered and subject to all the FATF recommendations that apply to banks and nonbank financial institutions;
- Regarding wire transfers, countries should require financial institutions, including money remitters, to include accurate information pertaining to the originator (name/address/account number) on funds transfers;
- Countries should review the adequacy of laws and regulations that relate to entities that are commonly abused for the purposes of financing terrorism, especially nonprofit and charitable organizations.[15]

Under the International Emergency Economic Powers Act and the Trading with the Enemy Act, the president of the United States can direct financial institutions to freeze the assets and block the accounts of persons and organizations belonging to designated hostile or renegade countries. For example, on January 23, 1995, President Clinton ordered that the assets of thirty Arab and Israeli groups be frozen in an attempt to prevent terrorists from using the American banking system. In late 1994, Israel sentenced Mohammed Salah, a used-car salesman from Bridgeview, Illinois, for carrying orders and thousands in cash to Hamas leaders in Israel. After the terrorist attack on September 11, 2001, President Bush signed executive order 13224 under the authority of the Emergency Economic Powers Act (50 U.S.C. 1701 *et seq.*). In declaring a national emergency due to the continued threat of catastrophic attack, the Executive Order blocked all property and interests in property of terrorist-related individuals and entities designated under the order. Initially the assets of twenty-seven individuals and organizations associated with the attacks were blocked, but by June 10, 2002, the list of blocked terrorist organizations, individuals, and their supporters had grown to 210. The 2002 National Money Laundering Strategy noted that 160 countries had blocking orders in force and that the vast majority of all nations had expressed cooperation with the campaign to thwart terrorist financing. In fact, the 2002 Money Laundering Strategy prioritizes the deployment of diplomatic resources to foster international cooperation and the sharing of resources and intelligence, with notable efforts utilizing the Egmont Group of FIUs, of which FinCEN is a part.[16]

SECURING U.S. BORDERS

In the age of color-coded terrorist alerts and the reintroduction of small-pox vaccinations, border security and homeland defense have become a national security imperative. The U.S.'s land and sea border stretches 9,600 miles—the largest undefended border in the world. In 1996, more than 400 million people entered the United States (most as visitors), up from 225 million in 1980. About 1.6 million enter the United States every year and stay—although no one knows for sure, perhaps half that number are illegal migrants. Approximately 5 million commercial trucks arrive from Mexico and Canada, and 4 million ocean containers enter the United States every year through its 361 sea and river ports—about 95 percent of U.S. international trade.[17] In short, the borders of the United States are porous and easily circumvented by transnational criminals who smuggle all manner of contraband, including narcotics, illegal migrants, chlorofluorocarbons, stolen vehicles and art, endangered species, and perhaps biological, chemical, and radiological weapons. Determined terrorists, who may be legal or illegal migrants, are extremely difficult to identify and intercept.

In the wake of the September 2001 terrorist attacks, the focus on people crossing into the United States became paramount in U.S. efforts to fight transnational crime. In December 2001, the United States and Canada reached an agreement that placed 400 National Guard troops at 43 border crossings and deployed military aircraft to patrol the 4,000-mile border. U.S. Attorney General John Ashcroft announced that there would be more integrated border enforcement teams, a coordination of visa policies, joint training of airline personnel, and an increase in shared intelligence between the two countries. Also in December 2001, the two countries signed a "smart border" declaration, pledging to use biometric identifiers such as fingerprints, voice recognition, and retina scans in travel documents to make it easier to identify people who have been cleared through the screening process.[18]

Key points of entry into the United States are typically overwhelmed with illegal entrants for which there are no adequate detention space. These aliens must then be released on parole, fail to appear for scheduled hearings, and simply vanish into the general population. New immigration and alien visitation policies have been implemented to address this problem. For example, in January 2003, a new immigration rule was proposed that would require commercial transportation companies to submit detailed manifests of all passengers and crewmembers to the federal government before an aircraft or other vessel departs or arrives in the United States. The rule went into effect in February 2003 as a part of the Enhanced Border Security and Visa Entry Reform Act of 2002. The immigrant fingerprinting and registration program administered by the INS requires all male visitors sixteen and older from Iran, Iraq, Syria, Libya, and Sudan to register with the government by December 16, 2002. On January 10, 2003, the requirement was extended to foreign visitors from twelve additional countries: Afghanistan, Algeria, Bahrain, Lebanon, Morocco, North Korea, Oman, Qatar, Somalia, Tunisia, United Arab Emirates, and Yemen.[19]

The first line of defense against alien smuggling lies at sea. In 1996 alone, the Coast Guard intercepted over 9,000 migrants. After the September 11 terrorist attacks, the Coast Guard began requiring ninety–six-hour advance notice of arrival of all vessels heading to U.S. ports. Small elite marine teams have been deployed to respond to any suspicious activity involving incoming vessels (some intelligence has suggested that terrorists might try to users divers to plant explosives at or near port facilities). The U.S. Customs Service has delivered gamma-ray technology to ports around the country to scan containers for radiological materials. Customs has also begun checking some incoming vessels offshore or in foreign ports. In February 2003, customs began requiring sea carriers to provide details about the contents of shipping containers twenty-four hours before the cargo is loaded onto ships at foreign ports. The United States also provides model legislation to other countries, conducts overseas training for immigration and border patrol officials, and provides automated visa "lookout" systems to source countries.[20]

One of the more hopeful developments is the application of increasingly sophisticated surveillance and identification technologies used to patrol borders and monitor people. In October 2002, Attorney General Ashcroft unveiled the Gateway Information Sharing Project (ISI), a pilot program that integrates investigative information from federal, state, and local law enforcement that will be available to all participating agencies via the Internet. Investigators will be able to enter names, addresses, phrases, automobile makes, scars, and tattoos to retrieve information from other cases under investigation. In a test run, names from a drug case were entered randomly, whereupon it was revealed within seconds that a suspect was being investigated for mail fraud by another agency; previously, such a search might have taken six months.[21]

Border security has grown far beyond mere infrared/night scopes to include hidden seismic, metallic, and infrared sensors; biometric identification systems and databases; and high energy x-ray imaging equipment that allow inspectors to more easily and expeditiously probe the contents of shipping containers and trucks. Low Earth Orbit (LEO) data communications and Global Positioning System (GPS) technologies offer a very useful way to address the problem of container security. The data communications delivery system is based on two-way intelligent LEO satellite communicators installed on the inside of containers. Satellite communicators can receive a GPS location fix every hour during transit and record the open/close status of cargo door sensors.[22] By January 2003, eleven of the world's busiest seaports had begun using an electronic container security system used by the U.S. military to keep track of overseas ammunition and supply shipments. Savi Technology of Sunnyvale, California, created the system, called Smart and Secure Tradelanes. The technology uses electronic tags/seals placed on cargo container closures. The seals send radio signals to a secure Internet site where monitors can determine the whereabouts and contents of individual containers, as well as whether or not containers have been opened. Through early 2003, deployment of the system had been modest: Only about one hundred containers equipped with electronic seals had been shipped from Hong Kong and Singapore to Seattle, Los Angeles, and Long Beach over the previous two months.[23]

A major component of border security is based on biometric technologies used to identify individuals by their unique physiological characteristics (finger, hand, iris, retina, and facial patterns—the patterns in irises are said to be even more reliable identifiers than fingerprints) and behavioral characteristics (voice, signature, and keystroke). Biometrics involves optical, thermal, and audio scanners used to record personal features. Mathematical algorithms reduce the information to digital data. At present, the U.S. government is compiling digital dossiers of the irises, fingerprints, voices, and faces of terrorist suspects. Researchers at Carnegie Mellon University and MIT, under the direction of the Defense Advance Research Projects Agency (DARPA), are using video cameras and computers to analyze how people walk to determine if their gait creates a unique "signature pattern" that can be used to identify individuals. The U.S. Biometrics Automated Toolset, or BAT, includes fifty laptops equipped with scanners. The information is stored in a central database at an unidentified U.S. intelligence agency. Both the FBI and INS have used BAT. An additional 400 laptops were prepared for the 2003 invasion of Iraq, where soldiers could even search the database via satellite phone from a battlefield location.

A new tool in this area is a product called FaceIt Argus, an automated system that allows each camera in a surveillance system to serve as an observation point, even when video is not being actively monitored. FaceIt scans 1 million faces per minute and can compare them with records in any database at rates of up to 60 million records per minute. INS and customs could integrate the FaceIt system with fingerprint and retinal scanners to provide detailed criminal histories. In May 2002, President Bush signed the Enhanced Border Security and Visa Entry Reform Act, legislation that required the State Department to issue visas and travel documents that are tamperproof and machine-readable using biometric identifiers. The law also requires that the INS install devices capable of scanning these biometric documents at all U.S. ports of entry by October 26, 2003. Ultimately, U.S. customs could use handheld scanners that interface with federal databases over a secure wireless network to almost instantaneously identify terrorists and other criminals.[24] Software used by casinos to catch gambling cheats may also be used to identify terrorists. NORA, or Non-Obvious Relationship Awareness, uses face recognition to match an image caught on a surveillance camera with a database of known cheaters (or terrorists). NORA is also used to evaluate information such as names, addresses, social security and credit card information, and other data that could be used to analyze possible relationships among people suspected of terrorism or associating with terrorists.[25]

Aside from biometrics, the United States is spending billions to increase the use of sophisticated technologies such as thermal imaging, unmanned aerial vehicles, and low-noise profile surveillance aircraft. In June 2002, the Coast Guard awarded an $11 billion contract to Lockheed Martin and Northrop Grumman to build a fleet of seventy-six unmanned surveillance aircraft. Such "drones" are and will continue to be widely used in anti-smuggling, antiterrorism, and drug interdiction operations.[26]

A plan emanating from Oak Ridge National Laboratory in Tennessee would place biological, chemical, and radiological weapons detectors at thousands of cell phone towers across the United States (30,000 exist). The program, called Sensor Net, would be linked by small computers that would detect an attack, compute how a weapons-plume would spread, and disseminate information nationwide to law enforcement and emergency personnel. Oak Ridge scientists have also designed a system called Aqua Sentinel to protect city drinking water. Aqua Sentinel uses algae to monitor the safety of drinking water. A massive algae kill could be detected within minutes, allowing for a drinking water system to be shut down before poisons could pass through. The Oak Ridge lab has also developed the "Boarding Pass Analyzer," a sophisticated mass spectrometer that reads specific molecular signatures of chemicals. The system can detect minute amounts of certain chemicals and explosives on airline boarding passes within seconds.[27]

THE USA PATRIOT ACT

In response to the September 11, 2001, terrorist attacks upon the United States, the Bush administration and the U.S. Congress passed the USA Patriot Act. Title III of the act contains significant new tools to combat money laundering and terrorist financing, in addition to expanding the government's legal authority to intercept communications and gather information.

To better understand the Patriot Act's surveillance and interception provisions, a brief overview of federal communications privacy law is in order. Federal communications privacy law consists of a three-tiered system. Title III of the Omnibus Crime Control and Safe Streets Act of 1968 gives law enforcement the power to secretly capture conversations when certain criminal offenses are suspected and senior Justice Department officials approve. At level two, 18 U.S.C. 2701-2709 protects telephone records, e-mail held in third-party storage, and the like. Investigators may access these records pursuant to a warrant or court order in connection with any criminal investigation and without the extraordinary levels of approval required under the aforementioned Title III. 18 U.S.C. 3121-3127 covers the third and least intrusive level regarding the government's use of trap and trace devices and pen registers (a kind of secret caller ID), which identify the source and destination of calls made to and from a particular phone. Orders for this third level of searching are based on the certification by the government that information relevant to the investigation of a crime may be obtained—no disinterested third party (court) finding is necessary. The Patriot Act expanded the government's authority to search at all three levels. The act:

- authorizes pen register and trap and trace orders for e-mail communications;
- authorizes nationwide execution of court orders for pen registers, trap and trace devices, and access to stored e-mail or communication records;
- legally treats stored voice mail like stored e-mail (as opposed to telephone conversations that require a probable cause search warrant);
- permits interception of communications to and from a trespasser within a computer system with the permission of the system's owner;
- adds terrorist and computer crimes to the predicate offenses under Title III of the Omnibus Crime Control and Safe Streets Act of 1968;
- encourages cooperation between law enforcement and foreign intelligence investigators;
- contains a sunset provision of December 31, 2005.[28]

The act also eases some of the restrictions on foreign intelligence gathering within the United States, while providing U.S. intelligence with greater access to information unearthed during a criminal investigation. The act:

- permits "roving surveillance"—court orders omitting the identification of the instrument, facility, or place where the surveillance is to occur if the court deems that the target is likely to thwart the surveillance;
- increases the number of judges on the Foreign Intelligence Surveillance Act (FISA) court from seven to eleven;
- establishes a claim against the United States for certain communications privacy violations by government personnel;
- expands the prohibition against FISA orders based solely on an American's exercise of his or her First Amendment rights.[29]

Title III of the Patriot Act also enhances the capability of law enforcement in its criminal and civil money laundering and asset forfeiture efforts. The 2002 National Money Laundering Strategy notes, however, that these provisions are not self-implementing and that the Department of the Treasury faces a considerable task in drafting and implementing regulations. Some significant provisions that were in effect as of the 2002 report were requiring anti–money laundering compliance programs at a broad range of financial institutions (including employee training, presence of at least one compliance officer, the development of internal policies, procedures, and controls, and an independent audit feature), prohibiting U.S banks from maintaining correspondent accounts for foreign shell banks (banks with no physical presence in the foreign country), developing a Suspicious Activity Report (SAR) reporting system for brokers and dealers in securities, money services businesses, and casinos (threshold reporting requirement: $5,000), having foreign correspondent banks identify their owners, providing FinCEN access to reports by nonfinancial trades and businesses where cash transactions exceeded $10,000 (thus, giving law enforcement access to information previously denied it), and fostering the exchange of information between financial institutions and the public and private sectors in the areas of money laundering and terrorist financing. This last provision in particular has been most controversial, as civil libertarians argue that it violates financial privacy. Section 314 of the Patriot Act now allows financial institutions to share information with one another after providing notice to the Treasury Department that suspicious activity has transpired. The financial institutions are required to maintain the confidentiality of information exchanged; however, regulations pursuant to the Patriot Act also gives FinCEN authority to ask financial institutions to search their records to determine whether that institution has engaged in transactions with specified individuals, entities, or organizations. Businesses that previously were required to report cash transactions of more than $10,000 to the IRS were now also required to file a SAR with the Department of the Treasury.

The Patriot Act authorizes the Secretary of the Treasury and the Attorney General to issue a summons or subpoena to any foreign bank that maintains a correspondent account in the United States. Law enforcement can request records related to correspondent accounts, including records maintained outside of the United States. Foreign banks are now required to appoint an agent authorized to accept service of legal process. Section 311 gives the Treasury Department the authority to not only obtain information about correspondent accounts, but terminate those accounts as well. Section 325 of the act gives the Treasury the authority (but does not require it) to regulate concentration accounts—accounts financial institutions use to aggregate funds from different clients' accounts for various transactions. Section 359 also brought informal banking systems, such as the hawala, under BSA reporting requirements.[30]

The Patriot Act creates new crimes and enhances the penalties for others. The law:

- outlaws laundering in the United States of any proceeds from foreign crimes of corruption or violence;

- prohibits laundering the proceeds from "Cybercrime" or supporting a terrorist organization;
- increases the penalties for counterfeiting;
- provides explicit authority to prosecute overseas fraud involving American credit cards;
- seeks to permit prosecution of money laundering in the place where the predicate offense occurs.

The Patriot Act also creates two new types of forfeitures and modifies some confiscation-related procedures. First, it allows the confiscation of all property of any individual or entity that participates in or plans an act of terrorism, as well as any property derived from or used to facilitate acts of terrorism. (Due process, double jeopardy, and ex post fact are all implicated here.) Property located in the United States may be confiscated for a wide range of crimes committed in violation of foreign law. The United States may also enforce foreign forfeiture orders.

Additional new crimes and supplements to existing law created by the Patriot Act relate to terrorist attacks on mass transportation facilities, biological weapons offenses, harboring terrorists, providing material support to terrorists, and fraudulent charitable solicitation. The act also increases the rewards for information in terrorist cases, permits nationwide and perhaps worldwide execution of warrants in terrorism cases, and allows the Attorney General to collect DNA samples from prisoners convicted of any federal crime of violence or terrorism. The act also contains a number of provisions meant to prevent alien terrorists from entering the country, especially from Canada, and to detain and deport alien terrorists and those who support them. The number of Border Patrol, INS, and customs agents was tripled at the Canadian border, and under the Patriot Act, $100 million was provided to improve INS and customs technology and to supply additional equipment for monitoring along the northern border.[31]

Privacy versus Security

As noted, the Patriot Act expands all four tools of law enforcement surveillance: wiretaps, search warrants, pen register/trap and trace orders, and subpoenas. It is in this respect that the act has been most controversial, raising numerous civil libertarian concerns. One of the more controversial provisions involves the Foreign Intelligence Surveillance Act (FISA) of 1978, which created a secret court that reviews FBI requests to investigate "agents of a foreign power" operating in the United States who are believed to be spying or furthering other transnational crimes such as terrorism. Seven judges approve requests in secret, with no published orders, opinions, or public records. Executive Order 12949, signed by President Clinton on February 9, 1995, authorized the Department of Justice to conduct physical as well as electronic searches without obtaining a warrant in open court, notifying the subject, or providing an inventory of items seized (all Fourth Amendment requirements). Under FISA and EO 12949, targets may include persons not suspected of a crime, who may be searched if probable cause exists that they are associated with enemies of the United States. Because of past abuses in which intelligence-gathering powers were used to spy on political enemies, Justice Department officials essentially created a barrier between the intelligence gathering and criminal investigation roles of the FBI. The Patriot Act removed that barrier, allowing for broader sharing of classified national security information with domestic criminal investigators. Under the act, the FBI can now apply for search warrants and wiretaps for law enforcement purposes "so long as a significant foreign intelligence purpose" remains. The powers granted to government under FISA now include that

- law enforcement need merely tell a judge that certain on-line information is "relevant" to an investigation, and they may spy on web-surfing activities of innocent American citizens, including items entered into search engines. The person being monitored need not be the target of the investigation, and the government is not obligated to report to the court or ever tell the person that they had been monitored;
- nationwide roving wiretaps permit the FBI and CIA to go from phone to phone and computer to computer without demonstrating that each is being used by a suspect or target of a court ordered search. The government may serve a single wiretap, pen/trap order, or FISA wiretap on any person or entity nationwide, whether or not that person or entity is specifically named in the order. The government is not required to show the court that information to be acquired is relevant to a criminal investigation, and in pen/trap or FISA searches, it need not even report where the order was served or what information was acquired;
- Internet Service Providers (ISPs) may voluntarily relinquish all noncontent information to law enforcement without a court order or subpoena. A subpoena minus court review is all that is required to access records of session times, means, and sources of payments and bank and credit card account numbers;
- the expansion of FISA authority increases the sharing of intelligence between law enforcement agencies and foreign intelligence entities, including the disclosure of previously secret criminal grand jury information.[32]

The Patriot Act has been subject to judicial review. In May 2002, the FISA Court itself refused to give the Justice Department broad new powers provided by the Patriot Act, citing abuses in which the FBI supplied erroneous information to the Court in over seventy-five search warrant and wiretap applications in just the previous two years. The judges also said that Justice Department authorities improperly shared classified intelligence information on at least four occasions. The Court said that rules proposed by Attorney General John Ashcroft would give prosecutors too much control over counterintelligence investigations and allow the government to misuse intelligence information in criminal cases. However, in November 2002, a special three-member secret appeals court met for the first time in FISA's twenty-four-year history, ruling that the government may conduct secret wiretaps and searches of U.S. citizens absent probable cause of criminal activity.[33]

In January 2003, the Fourth Circuit Court of Appeals ruled that the president has the authority to declare an individual an "enemy combatant" (or terrorist), whereupon that individual may be held in military custody indefinitely, without being charged or provided access to a lawyer. The decision overturned a lower court in the case involving Yaser Hamdi, a U.S. citizen accused of fighting for the Taliban in Afghanistan. In this case, the defendant was captured on foreign soil. In the related case of suspected "dirty bomber" Jose Padilla (the accused was nabbed at Chicago's O'Hare airport on suspicion of plotting to detonate a conventional bomb laced with radioactive materials), the courts have not ruled on the constitutionality of detaining American citizens as "enemy combatants" when they are seized in the United States.[34]

In addition to many Patriot Act provisions, recent government initiatives aimed at information gathering have huge privacy implications. DARPA is developing the Total Information Awareness system (TIA) to collect and analyze a gigantic database of information, including e-mail traffic, Internet use, credit-card purchases, and phone and bank records of foreign persons as well as U.S. citizens. TIA detractors refer to an Orwellian system where a dossier is maintained on every American. Supporters point to a subcomponent of TIA called Genisys, a feature designed to separate identity information from transactions conducted, with the association reformed only when evidence of wrongdoing and legal authority to do so exists.[35]

Because many ISPs lack the ability to discriminate communications to identify a particular subject's communications, the FBI developed a diagnostic tool called Carnivore. Carnivore gives the FBI the ability to intercept and collect electronic (e-mail) communications that are the subject of a lawful order. The program is similar to commercial "sniffers" and network diagnostic tools used by ISPs, except that it provides the ability to differentiate between communications that are lawful to intercept and those that are not. Under the authority of the Electronic Communications Privacy Act of 1986, Carnivore can legally collect transactional records through a court order, but without probable cause. Transactional records include the "to" and "from" lines in e-mail communications (but not the subject or "re" lines) and routing, billing, and other information maintained by the ISP. Searches of content would still require a search warrant based on probable cause that a crime has been committed. An unfortunate by-product of Carnivore may be that it provides an unacceptably high level of access to the data pipeline it monitors, thus providing a "backdoor" for spies and hackers intent on accessing computers, shutting down Web sites and company servers, or spreading computer viruses, all without being detected by ISP security systems necessarily disabled because of Carnivore installation.[36]

THE HOMELAND SECURITY ACT

In addition to the Patriot Act, another far-reaching piece of legislation enacted subsequent to the September 11 terrorist attacks was the Homeland Security Act that created the federal Department of Homeland Security in the executive branch of the U.S. government. The creation of the department combined twenty-two federal agencies, the largest reorganization of the federal government in over half a century. The primary mission of the department is to prevent terrorist attacks, with a specific emphasis on the following areas: (1) analysis and infrastructure protection; (2) chemical, biological, radiological, nuclear, and related countermeasures; (3) border and transportation security; (4) emergency preparedness and response; and (5) coordination with other parts of the federal government, with state and local governments, and with the private sector.

The Under Secretary for Information Analysis and Infrastructure Protection is responsible for receiving and analyzing law enforcement intelligence in order to identify terrorist threats within the United States. Other duties include analyzing the vulnerabilities of key resources and critical infrastructures, integrating information to identify priorities and protective measures, developing a comprehensive national plan to protect key resources and critical infrastructures, and administering the Homeland Security Advisory System responsible for exercising public threat advisories and providing specific warning information to state and local governments and the private sector.

The responsibilities of the Under Secretary for Chemical, Biological, Radiological, and Nuclear Countermeasures include securing people, infrastructures, property, resources, and systems from the stated threats; conducting a research and development program; procuring technology and systems for detecting, preventing, and responding to such terrorist threats; preventing the importation of such weapons and materials into the United States; and establishing guidelines for state and local governments to develop countermeasures in this area.

The Under Secretary for Border and Transportation Security is responsible for preventing the entry of terrorists and the instruments of terror into the United States; securing the borders, territorial waters, ports, terminals, waterways, and air, land, and sea transportation systems of the United States; administering the immigration and naturalization laws of the United States, including the establishment of rules governing the granting of visas, administering the customs laws of the United States; and ensuring the efficient flow of legitimate traffic and commerce in carrying out the aforementioned responsibilities.

The Under Secretary for Emergency Preparedness and Response is responsible for the federal government's response to terrorist attacks and major disasters, including working with other federal and nonfederal agencies to build a comprehensive national incident management system and a single coordinated national response plan. In addition to coordinating the overall response to terrorist attacks, this subdepartment directs the Domestic Emergency Response Team, the Strategic National Stockpile, the National Disaster Medical System, and the Nuclear Incident Response Team. In response to a nuclear incident, the Under Secretary is authorized to utilize certain elements of the Department of Energy and the Environmental Protection Agency.

Civil libertarians contend that the law allows the federal government to maintain extensive files on virtually every American. Also controversial was the insertion of the Cybersecurity Enhancement Act, which expands the ability of the government to obtain information from telecom and ISPs. Emergency provisions in the act allow officials to access e-mail and other private communications without a court order.[37]

Report Card

A January 2003 report issued by the Justice Department's inspector general's office faulted the INS for lax security and stated that the nation's 159 international airports remain vulnerable to foreign terrorists and smugglers largely due to INS deficiencies. In 1999, the inspector general's office reported a range of problems with the design, security, and communication systems at INS airport facilities used to screen millions of foreign visitors to the United States every year. Nine months after the September 2001 terrorist attacks, the report found that the INS had not only failed to address the problems observed back in 1999, but also that new deficiencies were evident. Investigators found inoperable alarms and cameras and security features that had been turned off, not monitored, or not been installed.[38]

Although the White House goal of having in place by January 2003 a system for screening all airport baggage had been implemented, serious holes in airport security remained obvious as of early 2003. A report by the Transportation Department's inspector general found problems with equipment meant to screen baggage, including monitors for explosives giving too many false positives.[39]

The Government Accounting Office (GAO) reported in February 2003 that government agents supplied with false identifications easily bypassed U.S. border guards, who failed to even inspect their fake papers. The fake driver's licenses and birth certificates used by the agents were manufactured on home computers with commercially available software. The undercover agents passed through various points of entry, including Miami International Airport, Port Angeles, Washington, and the district in San Diego directly adjacent to Tijuana, Mexico.[40]

On the positive side, the U.S. government and law enforcement agencies worldwide have executed scores of arrests of terrorists since the September 11 attacks, including the alleged 9-11 "mastermind," Khalid Sheikh Mohammed. Terrorist cells and individual terrorists have been apprehended in the United States as well, and worldwide many of the assets used to finance terrorism have been blocked, seized, or frozen. Although the vulnerabilities to attack are obvious, it is also true that the United States has not suffered another major terrorist attack since September 11, 2001. One may assume that this fact is not due to lack of desire on the part of terrorists. FBI director Mueller has stated that in the first fifteen months following September 11, 2001, nearly one hundred terrorist attacks were prevented worldwide.[41]

PROTECTING CRITICAL INFORMATION INFRASTRUCTURES

As noted in the previous chapter, a cyberterrorist attack has the potential to cripple the United States as surely as would a major chemical, nuclear, or biological attack—perhaps more so. Fortunately, a wide variety of tools and techniques exist to help defenders of information infrastructures control access to, monitor, and respond to network attacks. Computer firewalls seek to control access by filtering the types of outside users and digital processes permitted on a given information network. Encryption hardware and software increases the confidentiality and security of stored data and communications, while hardware cards can be installed in computers to provide authentication and ease the utilization of encryption. Computer security firms and information systems vendors develop "patches" to help network providers and users control access. Control of access by insiders include the use of passwords, challenge and response systems, biometric identifiers (retina scans, for example), and secure tokens. Simple programs and procedures can be used to create non-networked copies of valuable information, while off-site storage of such backups complicates the goals of attackers. Automated hardware and software tools can monitor the activity being performed on an information network, analyze the degree of threat being posed by a given activity using algorithms, filter data for later analysis, and notify network operators when suspicious activity is detected. A good example is the Automated Security Incident Measurement (ASIM) system used at the Air Force Information Warfare Center. It provides real-time warnings of suspicious activities on networks connected to the system based on known patterns of suspicious activity. Some technologies allow defenders to stop cyberattacks before real damage accrues. For example, most antivirus programs allow users to erase viruses before the system can continue operating. Monitoring systems are capable of detecting malicious activity and automatically modifying network operations to prevent outside access. Evaluation and assessment tools allow personnel to scan for vulnerabilities, repair or bolster weak points, and backtrack digital pathways to pinpoint the origin of attack. Proactive prevention of digital attacks has been more difficult, as new or modified techniques used by hackers are difficult to detect. As Internet-based digital attacks continue to exceed those from internal systems, companies have deployed "computer firewalls" to protect internal networks, and both private and public sector organizations increasingly use encryption to safeguard data and communications.[42]

Greg Rattray, an expert on protecting information infrastructures, states that organizations in the public and private sectors continue to create, use, and organize core activities around information networks and infrastructures created by outsiders with too little regard for security, while the proliferation of open networks makes efforts to control access to such infrastructures extremely difficult. Linkages between classified and unclassified systems have created a new area of vulnerability for U.S. national security organizations. Similarly, the interconnectivity of financial information could compromise a bank with perfectly adequate security measures because it is connected to a network with a weak link. The potential for "cascading" is very real; for example, a disruption to an information infrastructure because of electric power loss (whether from natural causes or a digital attack) could cause financial markets dependent on timely and reliable information to shut down.

The entities that provide and operate most key U.S. information infrastructures lie outside of the U.S. government, which means that national defensive efforts must assess and coordinate mechanisms across the private and public sectors. The tools for attacking information infrastructures and waging so-called cyber- or strategic-information warfare are widely accessible, inexpensive, and difficult to defend against. (Bulgarian high school students using a 286 processor perpetrated some of the most damaging computer viruses unleashed in the 1990s.) Rattray observes that the primary constraint on developing effective defensive strategies is not the lack of technological tools, but the cost and availability of human expertise to organize, manage, and update these tools in a constantly changing technological environment.[43]

Throughout the 1990s, awareness of the threat from cyberattacks and the vulnerability of information infrastructures precipitated a variety of threat assessments and response proposals. After the terrorist attacks at the World Trade Center in 1993 and the Murrah Building in Oklahoma City in 1995, President Clinton issued Presidential Decision Directive (PDD) 39, "U.S. Policy on Counterterrorism." An outgrowth of this directive was an inter-agency effort called the Critical Infrastructure Working Group (CIWG), a body that identified eight critical U.S. infrastructures and molded U.S. efforts in developing a plan for strategic information warfare defense. The CIWG identified numerous threats, including "malicious hackers, disgruntled insiders, organized criminals, foreign terrorists, and nation-states." CIWG efforts were used in Executive Order 13010, which created the Presidential Commission on Critical Infrastructure Protection (PCCIP) and the Infrastructure Protection Task Force (IPTF). The Justice Department assumed leadership of the IPTF, while the role of the department and the FBI remained central to efforts to establish critical infrastructure defenses throughout the 1990s. The findings of the PCCIP resulted in the formation of a National Security Council interagency group, which made recommendations to the president and precipitated PDD 63 in 1998. This directive called on federal, state, and local officials to coordinate efforts with the private sector in creating critical infrastructure protection efforts in the areas of telecommunications, banking, energy, water systems, transportation, and emergency services. With PDD 63, a single focal point was created for critical infrastructure protection at the highest level of government, the National Security Council (NSC). PDD 63 also identified lead governmental agencies with their specific areas of responsibility, ranging from the Department of Defense (national defense/military responses, conventional and digital) to the Environmental Protection Agency (the water supply). The FBI's National Infrastructure Protection Center is responsible for coordinating timely warnings of threats and comprehensive analyses, and law enforcement investigation and response. PDD 63 also addressed the need for response and recovery capabilities after large-scale cyberwarfare attacks. Computer incident and emergency response teams also exist in the private sector, perhaps most notably the Computer Emergency Response Teams Coordinating Center at Carnegie Mellon University.[44]

Yet with all of the congressional hearings, media attention, and PDDs, the broader governmental polices of the Clinton/Gore executive branch emphasized accessibility, adaptability, and competitiveness, with security against strategic information attack receiving low priority. Likewise, regulatory and legislative measures in the 1980s and 1990s in the area of telecommunications stressed issues such as commercial competition and decency standards with little concern for security—in short, measures that increased the difficulty of instituting national defenses of information infrastructures. Greg Rattray observes that outside of defense, intelligence, and law enforcement, U.S. government actors like the Federal Energy Regulatory Commission, the Federal Communications Commission, the Federal Aviation Administration, and the U.S. Congress actively pursued conditions that made instituting strategic information warfare defenses more difficult by the end of the 1990s than had previously been the case.

A 1999 FBI survey found that 19 percent of private sector organizations surveyed reported sabotage of data or networks, and 14 percent reported financial fraud. Survey results indicated that companies recognized the dangers from insiders but also viewed foreign involvement as a major concern, especially in the areas of corporate or government-sponsored espionage. Kessler and associates, an investigative consulting company, found that proprietary information theft increased over 100 percent from 1997 to 1999. Greg Rattray notes that perhaps the greatest weakness lies with the technology producers. Hardware and software products and the standard-setting activities of companies like Microsoft underpin the operation of advanced information infrastructures, yet this sector has consistently created products and established standards with weak security and easily recognizable and exploitable vulnerabilities. Lax security features of technologies built into advanced information infrastructures, including those used by the Department of Defense, are notoriously weak. Both the PCCIP and PDD 63 demonstrated a blatant disregard for security of private-sector technology producers. The confrontational relationship between private technology producers, entities concerned with Internet privacy, and U.S. government agencies with a leading role in developing a strategic information warfare defense have likewise compounded the nation's vulnerabilities. Similarly, the debate over encryption policy has distanced the government from private sector firms it must enlist in the development of cyberwarfare defenses. By the turn of the twentieth century, the U.S. governmental response to the threat of cyberwarfare lacked clarity, a fact manifested in the underdevelopment of organizational structures to address the problem.[45]

Encryption

The necessity of protecting vital information and communication systems has led to the creation of robust, virtually unbreakable digital encryption technologies. Encrypting data and communications is now easily accomplished and integrated into desktop applications and network services. Organized criminals and terrorists use encryption to thwart the interception of electronic messages, thus hindering criminal investigations, efforts to prevent catastrophic terrorist attacks, and the gathering of foreign intelligence vital to national security. Encryption technology is used to advance a variety of transnational crimes, including economic and military espionage, terrorism, child pornography, computer crime, drug trafficking, and various frauds and financial crimes. Ramzi Yousef, the mastermind of the 1993 World Trade Center bombing, the Italian Mafia, the Cali cartel, and the infamous CIA agent Aldrich Ames (convicted of espionage against the United States) all used cryptography to conceal their activities. Financial terrorists introduced a malicious code into nine financial systems in London that enciphered their data, later contacting the companies to extort money in exchange for the key to breaking the codes. Of course, the sale of encryption keys to U.S. enemies would allow access to critical information and communication systems.

When investigators encounter encrypted data, absent the key or consent, access can be difficult if not impossible. In February 1997, a Swiss student harnessed the power of 3,500 computers on the Internet to break a forty-eight-bit key. The combined computers achieved a search rate of 1.5 trillion keys per hour, while the "code was cracked" in thirteen days. New 128-bit keys are impossible to break using such "brute force" methods. Even if the power of the world's 260 million personal computers were combined, it would take 12 million times the age of the universe to obtain the key by random searching. The answer lies with "key recovery systems," whereby authorized persons can obtain access to the key needed to decrypt information. The key is recovered using information stored with the ciphertext together with information held by a trusted officer of a given organization or a third party. Of course, if the organization in question is criminal in nature and it possesses its own key recovery system absent an outside party, law enforcement would have to obtain the cooperation of the criminals to get the key.[46]

The "Magic Lantern" technology is part of a broad FBI project called "Cyber Knight." Magic Lantern would allow investigators to secretly install over the Internet eavesdropping software that records every keystroke on a suspect's computer. The secret key used in encryption software could thus be recorded without a user's knowledge, permitting investigators to access scrambled information and communications used to further criminal activity. Existing FBI monitoring requires "sneak and peak" warrants that allow agents to sneak into a target's home and install a device using a "key logger system." Magic Lantern could be installed over the Internet by tricking a person into opening an e-mail attachment or by exploiting weaknesses found in popular commercial software that hackers routinely use to break into computers.[47]

INTERNATIONAL CRIME CONTROL EFFORTS

The United States has invested much time and capital in the negotiation of Mutual Legal Assistance Treaties (MLATs), bilateral accords intended to foster prosecutions of crimes with international dimensions. MLATs and executive agreements have been particularly useful in regularizing international asset forfeiture cooperation among treaty partners. In general, MLATs strengthen procedures for international cooperation and create obligations and channels of communication for exchange of information and evidence in criminal investigations and proceedings. Unfortunately, cooperation tends to be slow and unwieldy, as typical requests for information must travel from the field operatives up through the Department of Justice, the Department of State, and on to the foreign country and then similarly back down through channels in the foreign nation. Additionally, aggressive unilateral efforts by the United States could actually undermine international cooperation facilitated by bodies such as the UN and the FATF. As of 1999, the United States had ratified MLATs with twenty-two jurisdictions. In cases where there is no treaty or executive agreement in place, the State Department may draft a case-specific agreement or letters rogatory, the traditional means of obtaining assistance from foreign courts.

The United States continues to pursue aggressive extradition treaties with foreign nations in an effort to deny safe haven to international criminals. The United States presently has extradition treaties with over 105 nations. In 1996, Congress amended federal law to provide for extradition to the United States of foreign nationals who committed crimes of violence against U.S. nationals outside the United States, even without an extradition treaty.

Bilateral maritime drug interdiction agreements provide standing authority for the United States and its foreign partners to board and search each other's vessels in international waters and pursue suspect vessels and aircraft into territorial waters and airspace. The United States is party to nineteen maritime drug interdiction agreements with South American, Central American, and Caribbean nations and overseas Caribbean territories.

The G-8 and the UN Crime Commission work with the Puebla Group, a body established in March 1996 that consists of Central and North American immigration officials, who work together in the areas of alien smuggling and related human rights violations. The United States is also the principal financier of the World Customs Organization (WCO), which has over 145 member nations. The WCO activities principally facilitate international trade, but also include interdicting international drug shipments, promoting anti-smuggling and anti–money laundering initiatives, combating commercial fraud, and responding to violations of intellectual property rights.

Cooperation with the private sector is an important part of efforts to limit international smuggling activities. For example, the Customs Service developed the Career Initiative Program and the Business Anti-Smuggling Coalition to enlist the aid of commercial carriers. Customs provides advice on how to secure shipping operations against smugglers, while private carriers provide valuable intelligence to federal officials.[48]

The Palermo/UN Convention on Transnational Organized Crime

The UN Convention on Transnational Organized Crime came into being at a high-profile signing ceremony in Palermo, Italy, in December 2000. The treaty has two main goals. One is to bridge the gap between international legal systems, a problem that has long hindered transnational criminal investigations. The second broad goal is to establish standards for domestic laws to effectively combat organized crime. Under the treaty, signatory governments pledge to criminalize activities committed by organized crime groups, including corruption and corporate offenses, enhance anti–money laundering efforts, expedite extradition proceedings, and generally improve international cooperation. The Palermo Convention also established a series of protocols aimed at combating specific crimes, including trafficking in women and children, the smuggling of migrants, and the traffic in illegal firearms.[49]

A Role for Interpol

With a current membership of 177 countries, Interpol has undergone dramatic changes in the last decade in response to the growing threat of transnational crime. Its principal challenge has been to develop a system that allows for the sharing and dissemination of information among the member states. Interpol also continues to explore initiatives to standardize how law enforcement agencies in different countries collect, analyze, store, and utilize evidence of criminal acts. Interpol's long-term goal is to create an extensive and accessible database of organized criminals and criminal organizations around the world. Interpol's Analytical Criminal Intelligence Unit uses state-of-the-art software to establish links between crimes and offenders and disseminate that information to member countries.[50]

The International Criminal Court (ICC)

The United Nations first recognized a need to establish an international criminal court in a 1948 General Assembly resolution. As originally envisioned, the primary purpose of an international criminal body would be to try persons charged with acts of genocide and crimes of similar gravity. Draft statutes were prepared in 1951 and 1953, but the General Assembly postponed consideration of the drafts until a definition of aggression could be agreed upon. Although the establishment of an ICC has been considered periodically since that time, no serious movement occurred until the outbreak of war and subsequent war atrocities in the former Yugoslavia in 1993. At its fifty-second session, the General Assembly decided to convene a diplomatic conference on the establishment of an ICC to be held in Rome in June–July 1998. That conference precipitated the Rome Statute of the International Criminal Court. Ratification of the statute creating the court is an ongoing process, but is one that the United States opposes. Issues related to national sovereignty, criminal definitions, and the incompatibility of the laws of different nations render the efficacy of the International Criminal Court as a tool in combating transnational organized crime doubtful.[51]

CONCLUSION

Efforts to combat transnational organized crime are extensive and include some international initiatives that the United States fully supports.

Recognition of the growing problems of human smuggling, the traffic in weapons, and the ever-changing manifestations of the money laundering process is a good beginning. Still, aggressive legislation such as the USA Patriot Act and the recommendations of international bodies like the Financial Action Task Force are not enough. Real threats to transnational criminals will require transnational political will and cooperation, elements of international crime control that remain noticeably absent.

CHAPTER 7

Summary and Conclusion

Networks of criminals who coordinate their illicit ventures across national borders are not a new phenomenon. The traffic in slaves, land and sea piracy, and the traffic in illicit drugs are activities dating back centuries. What is relatively new (aside from increased academic attention and formal recognition of the problem by the United Nations and the U.S. government) is the rapid proliferation of transnational crimes into new geographic areas, as well as a staggering range of criminal ventures. Transnational crimes documented in this book include narcotics trafficking; arms trafficking; cargo theft from trucks and shipping terminals; automobile theft; piracy on the high seas; art and antiquities theft; software piracy; the smuggling of illegal migrants; sexual slavery and transnational prostitution; pornography; traffic in human organs; smuggling toxic wastes and CFCs; traffic in exotic life forms and endangered species; money laundering; the violation of intellectual property rights; product counterfeiting; currency counterfeiting; industrial theft and economic espionage; various financial frauds and high-tech computer crimes; terrorism; traffic in nuclear, radiological, biological, and chemical weapons; cyberterrorism; kidnapping; pirating of music compact discs and digital video discs; sports bribery; securities fraud; smuggling of gems and gold; poaching of fish and other wildlife; and illegal dumping of toxic wastes. Although this work has focused on transnational crime and the United States, dozens of countries around the world have documented large-scale and transnational organized crime.

The explosion of transnational crime in the latter decades of the twentieth century has been due to a variety of factors, including high profits driven by prohibition laws, the increasing global demand for illicit goods and services, state failures and civil wars, and economic liberalization and globalization. Liberalization and the opening of borders has undeniably encouraged and facilitated illicit sectors of the global economy. For example, social disruptions from economic reforms in Mexico have provided the impetus for increased opium and marijuana cultivation as well as new customers for migrant smugglers. Similarly, financial liberalization has made the movement and laundering of money easier, while practices like tax amnesties on repatriated capital attracts legal capital but also encourages launderers. Likewise, the growth in cross-border traffic arising from free trade measures has made conditions increasingly amenable to smugglers who conceal their goods among legal cargo. (Still, Peter Andreas and Michael Levi have noted that the causal connection between economic liberalization and globalization and the growth of transnational crime is not all that clear. In fact, they say that in some ways, the opening of economic borders has actually inhibited transnational crime. For example, economic liberalization has reduced the incentive to smuggle legal commodities.)[1] Another primary reason for the spread of transnational crime is the lack of political will to stop it. In fact, the profits from crime are so great, public officials and other powerful elites have, in many cases, been thoroughly corrupted. Some nation-states have been and remain the sponsors of terrorism and transnational organized crime. At present, transnational crime is perhaps best characterized as a "political-criminal nexus," defined as the fusion of political and criminal power.

THE INTERNATIONAL CRIME CONTROL STRATEGY

Presidential Decision Directive 42 (PDD-42) issued October 21, 1995, ordered executive branch agencies to increase their priority and resources devoted to the effort to combat international crime, specifically recognizing the national security implications of the phenomenon. The first International Crime Control Strategy of the United States was released in May 1998 and included the following goals:

- Goal 1: Extend the First Line of Defense Beyond U.S. Borders
- Goal 2: Protect U.S. Borders by Attacking Alien Smuggling and Smuggling-Related Crimes
- Goal 3: Deny Safe Haven to International Criminals
- Goal 4: Counter International Financial Crime
- Goal 5: Prevent Criminal Exploitation of International Trade
- Goal 6: Respond to Emerging International Crime Threats

- Goal 7: Foster International Cooperation and the Rule of Law
- Goal 8: Optimize the Full Range of U.S. Efforts[2]

THE UNITED STATES' FIRST INTERNATIONAL CRIME THREAT ASSESSMENT

Fast on the heels of the president's International Crime Control Strategy came the first ever International Crime Threat Assessment, released by the White House in December 2000. The sweeping assessment was developed by a U.S. government interagency working group pursuant to the president's International Crime Control Strategy. The assessment begins by noting the role the post–Cold War landscape and the opening of political and economic borders has played in precipitating the growth of transnational crime on a global scale. Especially significant are the advances in information and communication technologies that allow criminals to obtain, process, and protect information in order to evade law enforcers. The interactive capabilities of modern computer and telecommunication systems allow organized criminals to plot market strategies for illicit commodities, to identify the most efficient routes for smuggling and money laundering, and to create decoys and false trails for investigators and banking security. The more sophisticated criminal organizations now use surveillance technologies to track law enforcement activities and for counterintelligence.

Transnational crime groups seem to be networking and coordinating their ventures more so than in the past, sharing information, resources, and market access according to the principle of comparative advantage. Such cooperation has allowed gangs to merge expertise, reduce risks, and expand the scope of their activities. The major international criminal gangs are highly diversified, expanding into a broad range of illicit as well as legitimate businesses. Many of the larger criminal organizations have established business-like structures, including front companies and quasi-legitimate firms in order to facilitate and provide cover for their illegal enterprises. The typical transnational crime firm is now more professional, taking advantage of technological advances and employing specialists to enhance the efficiency of their operations. For example, major smuggling organizations use transportation specialists and legal experts to research commercial flows and learn about tariff laws and administrative procedures in commercial ports, while financial experts and banking insiders are used to identify emerging money laundering mechanisms, manage investments, and establish fronts. Lawyers manipulate the law and the judicial system to thwart investigations and prosecutions and shape legislation.

Another sinister development in recent years has been the increasing movement of terrorists and other extremist groups into organized crime activities. While these groups used organized crime (especially drug trafficking) to finance their insurgencies in the past, the collapse of the Soviet Union and the end of the Cold War eliminated a major source of funding—state sponsors. For example, Marxist insurgents in Colombia, unable to rely on Soviet or Cuban aid since the late 1980s, have turned to the drug trade for financing. The Revolutionary Armed Forces of Colombia (FARC) taxes and protects the cocaine trade in that country, while in Angola and Sierra Leone the costs of insurgency are paid for by mining and illegally exporting diamonds. Political, ideological, and religious terrorists also develop relationships with organized crime groups to acquire weapons, encryption software and global positioning equipment, and important contacts such as immigration officials, corrupt law enforcers, and money launderers.

The 2000 International Crime Threat Assessment also catalogs the principal transnational crimes affecting the United States and overviews transnational crime as it exists in various regions of the world. The report states that drug trafficking and international terrorism most directly threaten American lives and property. Other principal areas of transnational criminal activity identified include illegal migration, the worldwide traffic in women and children, environmental crimes, the illicit transfer of products across international borders, economic trade crimes such as piracy, the smuggling of contraband, the violation of intellectual property rights, industrial theft and foreign corrupt business practices, and financial crimes such as counterfeiting monetary instruments and currency and money laundering.

The principal threat from Western Europe are Italian criminal organizations, which maintain an active presence in the United States and are involved in extortion, gambling, counterfeiting, money laundering, drug trafficking, arms smuggling, and financial frauds. U.S. law enforcement believes that the Sicilian Mafia remains the most active Italian organized crime group in the United States and that it maintains close contact with American Cosa Nostra families in cities around the country. 'Ndrangheta, Camorra, and Sacra Corona groups also operate in the United States, particularly in Florida. From Eastern Europe, the principal threat to the United States is from Russian-based crime groups, considered to be among the best in the world in perpetrating economic and financial crimes. Although small groups of Russian criminals established footholds by the late 1970s, large-scale and sophisticated gangs with transnational dimensions and contacts in Russia moved into the United States after the dissolution of the Soviet Union in 1991. Although not considered to be as significant a threat as La Cosa Nostra, the assessment concludes that the Russians are well positioned to continue their criminal expansion in the United States. The report also notes that Albanian criminal syndicates are moving into the northeastern United States.

Southern Asia and China are a major source of the transnational criminal threat to the United States. Since the early 1990s, more than half of the heroin produced in Myanmar (Burma) is trafficked through Yunnan Province in China on its way to drug markets in North America and Australia. China is the leading violator of U.S. intellectual property rights, and factories in Guandong Province are significant producers of counterfeit and pirated goods. Chinese Triads in Hong Kong, Macau, and Taiwan, along with other crime groups in mainland China, have extended their criminal activities and developed relationships with ethnic Chinese crime groups in the United States. The Chinese syndicates perpetrate a broad range of crimes, including drug trafficking, alien smuggling, arms trafficking, money laundering, credit card fraud, and software piracy. Taking advantage of Ottawa's immigration policies, criminals have established Canada as the gateway for Chinese criminal activity directed at the United States. Hong Kong's two largest Triads, 14K and Sun Yee On, are involved in methamphetamine and heroin smuggling as well as alien smuggling into the United States, while the most dominant organized crime group in mainland China, the Big Circle Gang, is the source for much of the heroin and counterfeit credit cards smuggled into Canada and the United States.

The Yakuza, considered to be among the world's largest and most powerful criminal confederations, are thought to generate about $13 billion in annual revenue. Yakuza activity in the United States has been limited primarily to money laundering and financial frauds. U.S. law enforcement has noted that Yakuza groups have laundered money through the U.S. stock market and invested heavily in real estate, including golf courses and hotels. The Inagawa-Kai Yajuza group has invested heavily in Hawaii and the west coast states of the United States.

The center of transnational criminal activity originating from Africa is Nigeria. Pervasive corruption in Lagos has fostered powerful criminal syndicates that stretch into the far corners of the globe. According to U.S. customs data, 25 to 30 percent of the heroin seized at U.S. airports in recent years was seized from couriers working for Nigerian syndicates. Nigerian syndicates also specialize in various financial frauds, targeting primarily U.S. and United Kingdom businesses and private individuals. In East Africa, an increasing amount of U.S.-bound heroin has been appearing in Kenya, while Sudan remains a safe haven for international terrorists.

Colombian traffickers are responsible for supplying most of the world's finished cocaine, with the majority going to the United States. In fact, Colombia, Venezuela, and Ecuador are the primary staging areas for drugs exported to the United States. Colombia also is the leader in manufacturing counterfeit U.S. currency. Elsewhere in South America, the Andean countries of Peru and Bolivia are major sources of coca, while Venezuela is a major transshipment corridor for drugs trafficked through the Caribbean and destined for the United States. Bolivia is also a major staging area for the movement of illegal migrants from China and the Middle East to the United States. Authorities estimate that patent and trademark infringements in Argentina and Brazil cost U.S. firms $500 million in lost sales every year. The numerous island and cays as well as large stretches of open water make the Caribbean a major transshipment route for the passage of drugs, illegal migrants, arms, and contraband. Jamaica, the largest exporter of marijuana in the Caribbean, has well-established crime gangs with ties in Colombia and the United States, while Puerto Rico sits at the middle of three trans-Caribbean smuggling routes. This is an ideal locale because, once smuggled into the island, drugs and other contraband can be moved to the U.S. mainland easily. Customs officials do not generally restrict ships and planes. With criminal cells in the eastern U.S. seaboard, Dominican traffickers dominate the shipment of cocaine and marijuana from Puerto Rico to the United States. Caribbean nations also remain major offshore banking centers used for money laundering and income tax evasion.

Panama is a major offshore banking center, with money laundered through the Colon Free Zone estimated at $1 billion to $4 billion annually, much of it through the Black Market Peso exchange. Panama and other Central American countries serve as conduits for the shipment of drugs and other contraband, from points south up through Mexico and on to the United States. Mexico and the countries of Central America are by far the largest source of illegal migrants to the United States. Many of the migrants are from the region, primarily Honduras, Guatemala, Honduras, and Mexico; tens of thousands of others from India, China, and other Asian, African, and Middle Eastern countries are smuggled through Central America and Mexico annually. The U.S. government estimates that alien smuggling networks in Central America generate about $1 billion a year in gross annual revenue. Mexican drug traffickers corrupt public officials and exploit the huge amount of legitimate traffic along the porous U.S./Mexico border. Mexican traffickers dominate the U.S. methamphetamine market, while approximately half of the cocaine smuggled into the United States crosses the Southwest border. The smuggling of stolen vehicles, firearms, tobacco, alcohol, pirated goods, and illegal migrants are also common along the Mexican border.

On the flip side, the United States, with the world's largest and most diversified economy, provides an excellent environment for the transnational crime originating within its borders. The United States is a leading source of the world's contraband luxury goods (especially automobiles), firearms, tobacco products, and alcohol. While the United States is the world's largest drug importer, it is also a leading producer and exporter of marijuana, crack cocaine, and methamphetamines. In addition, the United States is a major transshipment point for contraband shipped from one foreign nation to another and is a significant source of precursor chemicals used in the global drug traffic. Both the complexity and strength of the U.S. economy keeps the nation as an attractive target for money launderers. Homegrown crime groups perpetrate a broad range of transnational crimes across the globe. The principal groups originating in the United States with transnational dimensions are some of the U.S.'s outlaw motorcycle gangs and, of course, the American La Cosa Nostra.

THE FUTURE OF TRANSNATIONAL ORGANIZED CRIME

The 2000 International Crime Threat Assessment concluded with somber predictions. The interagency working group suggested that the erosion of state authority and the process of globalization over the following ten years would result in the further diversification of transnational crimes, more directly impacting U.S. strategic interests. Large criminal syndicates such as the Sicilian Mafia, the Chinese Triad societies, and the Russian Mafiya will continue to pose a major threat to U.S. interests and will likely become more self-sufficient by 2010. The experts on the working group suggested that the cooperation among large criminal syndicates seen at the end of the twentieth century could be replaced by fully integrated transnational crime groups. Another possibility is that large interactive networks of smaller crime groups might cooperate and specialize in specific criminal activities. The assessment concluded that law enforcement would be challenged by increasing threats from individuals and small groups of criminals that utilize high-tech computer skills and telecommunications—electronic theft and the manipulation of financial markets were cited as credible threats. Transnational criminals are also likely to take advantage of scientific and manufacturing advances to produce new synthetic drugs and high-quality counterfeit products. Finally, while illegal enterprises such as drug trafficking, alien smuggling, the traffic in women and children, and other traditional rackets will continue, transnational organized crime groups are expected to be an even greater threat with regard to national security issues. The interagency working group fears an increasing role for organized crime groups in the brokering of illicit arms and weapons of mass destruction to foreign armies, militias, and terrorists, while crime groups and individuals are expected to become proficient at exploiting computer networks that control vital information infrastructures.[3]

Notes

CHAPTER 1

1. Roy Godson, William J. Olson, and Louise Shelly, eds., "Political Criminal Nexus," *Trends in Organized Crime* 3.1 (1997): 4.

2. David Pryce-Jones, "Corruption Rules the World," *The American Spectator*, December 1997, 22–25.

3. Michael D. Lyman and Gary W. Potter, *Organized Crime*, 2d ed. (Upper Saddle River, N.J.: Prentice-Hall, 2000).

4. Brian Freemantle, *The Octopus: Europe in the Grip of Organized Crime* (London: Orion, 1995).

5. Alex P. Schmid, "Links Between Transnational Organized Crime and Terrorist Crimes," *Transnational Organized Crime* 2.4 (1996): 41–81.

6. Douglas Keh and Graham Farrell, "Trafficking Drugs in the Global Village," *Transnational Organized Crime* 3.2 (1997): 90–110; Phil Williams, "Cooperation Among Criminal Organizations," *Transnational Organized Crime and International Security*, ed. Mats Berdal and Monica Serrano (Boulder, Colo.: Lynne Rienner Publishers, 2002).

7. "Russian Organized Crime Implicated in Figure Skating Scandal," 21 August 2002, http://www.cnn.com.

8. "Music Chiefs Warn of Piracy Threat," 21 January 2001, http://www.cnn.com.

9. Charles Feldman and Stan Wilson, CNN Los Angeles Bureau [no title], 21 March 2002, http://www.cnn.com.

10. "Police Say Suspect Confesses to Bali Bombing," 22 November 2002, http://www.cnn.com.

11. Bill Mears, "Colombia Paramilitary Leader Indicted," 24 September 2002, http://www.cnn.com.

12. "U.S. Prosecutors File Charges Against Members of Colombian Rebel Group," 13 November 2002, http://www.cnn.com.

13. "International Ringleader Sought after Record Ecstasy Bust in the U.S.," 27 July 2000, http://www.cnn.com.

14. "San Diego Gang Members Indicted in Connection with Cardinal's Murder," 11 February 1998, http://www.cnn.com.

15. "International Police Unit Cracks Crime Family in Canada," 16 July 1998, http://www.cnn.com.

16. "More Mafia Indictments in New York," 6 September 2002, http://www.cnn.com.

17. United States, House Subcommittee on Finance and Hazardous Materials, Committee on Commerce, *Testimony of Richard H. Walker, Director, Enforcement Division of the SEC*, 13 September 2000, http://www.sec.gov/news/testimony/ts142000.htm.

18. "Russian Money Laundering Probe Widens as First Charges Filed," 6 October 1999, http://www.cnn.com.

19. "U.S. Customs Seize $11 Million in Outbound Smuggled Cash," 24 August 2000, http://www.cnn.com.

20. "Child Smuggling Ring Broken, INS Says," 12 August 2002, http://www.cnn.com.

21. "U.N.: Child Sex Trade a Form of Terrorism," 17 December 2001, http://www.cnn.com.

22. "Nearly 8,000 Arrested in Alien Smuggling Scheme," 27 June 2001, http://www.cnn.com.

23. "Chinese Smuggling Ring Said to Have Used Indian Reservation," 14 December 1998, http://www.cnn.com.

24. Richard Stenger, "Report: Russian Mob Threatens Prime Fishery," 12 December 2001, http://www.cnn.com.

25. "Gangs Net Millions from Software Piracy," 6 May 1999, http://www.cnn.com.

26. "Brothers Guilty in Charlotte Terror Trial," 25 June 2002, http://www.cnn.com.

27. "U.S. Infrastructure Information Found on al-Qaeda Computers," 27 June 2002, http://www.cnn.com.

28. P.N. Grabosky, "Crime in Cyberspace," *Transnational Organized Crime* 4.3–4 (1998): 195–208.

29. Joseph Albini, R.E. Rogers, Victor Shabalin, Valery Kutushev, Vladimir Moiseev, and Julie Anderson, "Russian Organized Crime: Its History, Structure, and Function," *Journal of Contemporary Criminal Justice* 11.4 (1995): 213–43.

30. Chris Eskridge and Brandon Paeper, "The Mexican Cartels: A Challenge for the 21st Century," *Criminal Organizations* 12.1–2 (1998): 5–15.

31. Lyman and Potter, 2000.

32. Phil Williams, "Problems and Dangers Posed by Organized Transnational

Crime in the Various Regions of the World," *The United Nations and Transnational Organized Crime*, ed. Phil Williams and Ernesto U. Savona (London: Frank Cass, 1996).

33. Freemantle, 1995.

34. Julie Salzano and Stephen W. Hartman, "Cargo Crime," *Transnational Organized Crime*, 3.1 (1997): 39–49.

35. "The Changing Faces of Organized Crime," *Crime and Justice International* 13.10 (1997): 22.

36. Salzano and Hartman, 39–49.

37. Phil Williams, ed., *Illegal Migration and Commercial Sex: The New Slave Trade*, (London: Frank Cass, 1997).

38. Jennifer Clapp, "The Illicit Trade in Hazardous Wastes and CFCs: International Responses to Environmental Bads," *Trends in Organized Crime* 3.2 (1997): 14–18.

39. Donovan Webster, "The Looting and Smuggling and Fencing and Hoarding of Impossibly Precious, Feathered, and Scaly Wild Things," *Trends in Organized Crime* 3.2 (1997): 9–10.

40. "International Crime Threat Assessment," *Trends in Organized Crime* 5.4 (2000): 32–145.

41. Phil Williams, "Money Laundering," *Criminal Organizations* 10.4 (1997): 18–27.

42. *Patterns of Global Terrorism, 2001,* 13 May 2003, http://www.state.gov.

43. Rensselaer Lee, "Recent Trends in Nuclear Smuggling," *Transnational Organized Crime*, 2.4 (1996): 109–21.

44. Lyman and Potter, 2000.

45. United States, Hearing before the Subcommittee on International Security, International Organizations and Human Rights of the Committee on Foreign Affairs, House of Representatives, 103rd Congress, 1st Session, *The Threat of International Crime* (Washington, D.C.: GPO, 1993); United States, Hearing before the Committee on International Relations, House of Representatives, 104th Congress, 2nd Session, *Global Organized Crime* (Washington, D.C.: GPO, 1996).

46. "International Crime Control Strategy," *Trends in Organized Crime*, 4.1 (1998).

47. *Trends in Organized Crime*, 5.4 (2000).

48. Gerhard O.W. Mueller, "Transnational Crime: Definitions and Concepts," *Transnational Organized Crime* 4.3–4 (1998): 13–21.

49. Ibid., 14.

50. Ibid.

51. Mueller, 1998.

52. Peter Lupsha, "Transnational Organized Crime versus the Nation State," *Transnational Organized Crime* 2.1 (1996): 21–48.

53. Ibid.

54. Ibid.

55. Louis Roniger and S.N. Eisenstadt, "Patron-Client Relations as a Model of Structuring Social Exchange," *Society for Comparative Study of Society and History* (The Truman Research Institute, 1980).

56. Steffen W. Schmidt, *Friends, Followers, and Factions: A Reader in Political Clientelism* (Berkeley: University of California Press, 1977), xx.

57. Alan A. Block, *Masters of Paradise* (New Brunswick, N.J.: Transaction, 1991), 4.

58. Pino Arlachi, *Mafia Business: The Mafia Ethic and the Spirit of Capitalism* (New York: Verso, 1987); Anton Blok, *The Mafia of a Sicilian Village, 1860–1960* (New York: Harper and Row, 1974); Henner Hess, *Mafia and Mafioso: The Structure of Power* (Lexington, Mass.: D.C. Heath, 1973).

59. Joseph Albini, *The American Mafia: Genesis of a Legend* (New York: Appleton-Century Crofts, 1971).

60. Lupsha, 1996, 33.

61. Ibid.

CHAPTER 2

1. For the history of La Cosa Nostra in America, readers should begin with the following: Joseph Albini, *The American Mafia: Genesis of a Legend* (New York: Appleton-Century Crofts, 1971); Alan A. Block, *East Side–West Side: Organizing Crime in New York, 1930–1950* (New Brunswick, N.J.: Transaction, 1983); Stephen Fox, *Blood and Power* (New York: William Morrow, 1989); Humbert Nelli, *The Business of Crime: Italians and Syndicate Crime in the United State* (New York: Oxford University Press, 1976).

2. William Howard Moore, *The Kefauver Committee and the Politics of Crime* (Columbia, Mo.: University of Missouri Press, 1974).

3. Jay Albanese, *Organized Crime in America*, 3rd ed. (Cincinnati: Anderson, 1996).

4. Howard Abadinsky, *Organized Crime*, 6th ed. (Chicago: Nelson Hall, 2000).

5. Nelli, 1976.

6. The Pennsylvania Crime Commission, *Organized Crime in PA: A Decade of Organized Crime* (St. David's, Penn.: Commonwealth of PA, 1980).

7. Alan A. Block, *The Business of Crime* (Boulder, Colo.: Westview Press, 1991).

8. New York State Organized Crime Task Force, *Corruption and Racketeering in the New York City Construction Industry* (New York: New York University Press, 1990); Block, 1991; Abadinsky, 2000.

9. Abadinsky, 2000.

10. Pennsylvania Crime Commission, 1980.

11. Ibid.

12. *Crime and Justice International*, 13.10 (1997).

13. "Crackdown Shows Mob's Wall Street Role," *Tribune Review* [Pittsburgh], 15 June 2000: A5.

14. Stephen Pizzo, Mary Fricker, and Paul Muolo, *Inside Job* (New York: McGraw-Hill, 1989).

15. Patrick J. Ryan, *Organized Crime: A Reference Handbook* (Santa Barbara, Calif.: ABC-CLIO, Inc., 1995).

16. James B. Jacobs, Christopher Panarella, and Jay Worthington, *Busting the Mob: U.S. v. Cosa Nostra* (New York: New York University Press, 1994).

17. The Pennsylvania Crime Commission, *Organized Crime: A Decade of Change* (Conshohocken, Penn.: Commonwealth of PA, 1990).

18. Jacobs, et al., 1999.

19. Alan A. Block, "On the Origins of Fuel Racketeering: The Americans and the Russians in New York," *Transnational Organized Crime* 2.2–3 (1997): 156–75.

20. Potter and Lyman, 2000.

21. Pennsylvania Crime Commission, 1990.

22. President's Commission on Organized Crime, *The Impact: Organized Crime Today* (Washington, D.C.: GPO, 1986).

23. Pennsylvania Crime Commission, 1990.

24. Potter and Lyman, 2000.

25. Pennsylvania Crime Commission, 1990; Lyman and Potter, 2000.

26. Pennsylvania Crime Commission, 1990.

27. Ibid.

28. Lyman and Potter, 2000; Pennsylvania Crime Commission, 1990.

29. Ibid.

30. Alex Frew McMillan, "Black Economy 4.5% of Japan's Output," 25 May 2001, http://www.cnn.com.; James R. Richards, *Transnational Criminal Organizations, Cybercrime, and Money Laundering: A Handbook for Law Enforcement Officers, Auditors, and Financial Investigators* (Boca Raton, Fla.: CRC Press, 1999).

31. Lyman and Potter, 2000.

32. Martin Booth, *The Triads: the Chinese Criminal Fraternity* (London: Grafton, 1990); Mark Craig, "Best Practice in Intelligence Management with Respect to Chinese Organized Crime," *Trends in Organized Crime* 3.2 (1997): 62–66; Richards, 1999; Lyman and Potter, 2000.

33. Richards, 1999; Lyman and Potter, 2000.

34. Marianne Bray, "Foreign Triads Infiltrating China," 18 March 2002, http://www.cnn.com; Willy Wo–Lap Lam, "China Corruption Linked to Triads," 10 March 2002, http://www.cnn.com.

35. Joseph L. Albini, R.E. Rogers, Victor Shabalin, Valery Kutushev, Vladimir Moiseev, and Julie Anderson, "Russian Organized Crime: Its History, Structure, and Function," *Journal of Contemporary Criminal Justice* 11.4 (1995): 213–43; Phil Williams, ed., *Russian Organized Crime* (London: Frank Cass, 1997); James O. Finckenauer and Yuri Voronin, *The Threat of Russian Organized Crime* (Washington: National Institute of Justice, 2001); Todd S. Foglesong and Peter Solomon, Jr., *Crime, Criminal Justice, and Criminology in Post-Soviet Ukraine* (Washington: National Institute of Justice, 2001); William H. Webster, Arnaud de Borchgrave, and Frank J. Cilluffo, *Russian Organized Crime: Putin's Challenge*, Global Organized Crime Project (Washington: Center for Strategic and

International Studies, 2000); Christopher J. Ulrich and Timo A. Kivimaki, *Uncertain Security: Confronting Transnational Crime in the Baltic Sea Region and Russia* (Lanham, Md.: Lexington Books, 2002); Richards, 1999; Lyman and Potter, 2000; Abadinsky, 2000.

36. Richard L. Palmer, "The New Russian Oligarchy: The Nomenklatura, the KGB, and the Mafiya," *Trends in Organized Crime* 3.1 (1997): 8–14; Timothy M. Burlingame, "Criminal Activity in the Russian Banking System," *Transnational Organized Crime* 3.3 (1997): 46–72; Taras Kuzio, "Crime Still Ukraine's Greatest Enemy," *Trends in Organized Crime* 3.1 (1997): 27–30; Louise I. Shelley, "The Price Tag of Russia's Organized Crime," *Trends in Organized Crime* 3.1 (1997): 24–26.

37. Finckenauer and Voronin, 2001; Richards, 1999.

38. Block, 1997, Richards, 1999.

39. Finckenauer and Voronin, 2001; Richards, 1999.

40. Robert J. Nieves, "Breaking Drug Cartels: Lessons from Colombia," *Trends in Organized Crime* 3.3 (1998): 13–29; Sidney Jay Zabludof, "Colombian Narcotics Organizations as Business Enterprises," *Transnational Organized Crime* 3.2 (1997): 20–49; Robert J. Bunker and John P. Sullivan, "Cartel Evolution: Potentials and Consequences," *Transnational Organized Crime* 4.2 (1998): 55–74; Richards, 1999; Lyman and Potter, 2000.

41. Richards, 1999.

42. Stanley A. Pimentel, "Mexico's Legacy of Corruption," *Trends in Organized Crime* 4.3 (1999): 9–28; Chris Eskridge and Brandon Paeper, "The Mexican Cartels: A Challenge for the 21st Century," *Criminal Organizations* 12.1–2 (1998): 5–15; United States, Hearing before the Subcommittee on Crime of the Committee on the Judiciary, House of Representatives, Drug Trafficking on the Southwest Border, 107th Congress, 1st session (Washington, D.C.: GPO, 2001).

43. "Mexican Police Arrest Suspected Drug Kingpin," 10 March 2002, http://www.cnn.com.

44. "Bust May Mark End of Drug Kingpin Era," *Tribune Review* [Pittsburgh], 16 March 2003: A2.

45. *An Introduction to Organized Crime in the United States*, Organized Crime/Drug Branch, Criminal Investigative Division (Washington, D.C.: GPO, 1993); Richards, 1999; Potter and Lyman, 2000; Abadinsky, 2000.

46. Tom Behan, *The Camorra* (New York: Routledge, 1995); *An Introduction to Organized Crime in the United States*, 1993; Richards, 1999; Potter and Lyman, 2000.

47. Angiolo Pellegrini, "La 'Ndrangheta: Spunti di Situazione [The 'Ndrangheta: An Account of the Situation]. Direzione Investigativa Antimafia, Centro Operativo Reggio Calabria, translated in *Trends in Organized Crime* 3.2 (1997): 70–74; Richards, 1999; Potter and Lyman, 2000.

48. United States, Hearing before the Subcommittee on Africa of the Committee on International Relations, House of Representatives, *Combating International Crime in Africa* (Washington, D.C.: GPO, 1998); Mark M. Richard, Michael C.

Stenger, and Jonathan Winer, Prepared Statements before the Subcommittee on Africa of the House International Relations Committee, *Trends in Organized Crime* 3.2 (1997): 131–49; "The FBI Perspective" [on organized crime in the U.S.], *Crime and Justice International* 19.72 (2003): 13–16.

49. Potter and Lyman, 2000.

50. Department of the Solicitor General, Canada, 13 June 2002, http://www.sgc.gc.ca\Efact\eorgcrime.htm.

51. Criminal Intelligence Service Canada (*hereafter CISC*), *1996 Annual Report*, http://www.cisc.gc.ca.

52. M.E. Beare, *Criminal Conspiracies: Organized Crime in America* (Toronto: Nelson-Canada, 1996); Stephen R. Schneider, "Combating Organized Crime in (and by) the Private Sector: A Normative Role for Canada's Forensic Investigative Firms," *Journal of Contemporary Criminal Justice* 14.4 (1998): 351–67; CISC *Annual Reports*, 1996–2001.

53. Schneider, 1998.

54. Ibid.

55. CISC, *2001 Annual Report*.

56. CISC, *1997 Annual Report*.

57. CISC, *2001 Annual Report*.

58. CISC, *1999 and 2001 Annual Reports*.

59. CISC, *2001 Annual Report*.

60. CISC, *1997 and 1999 Annual Reports*.

61. CISC, *1998 and 1999 Annual Reports*.

62. CISC, *2000 Annual Report*.

63. CISC, *2001 Annual Report*.

64. CISC, *1998–2001 Annual Reports*.

65. CISC, *1996, 1999, 2000–2001 Annual Reports*.

66. CISC, *1996–1998 Annual Reports*.

67. Organized Crime Agency of British Columbia, *2001 Annual Report*; CISC, *1996–2001 Annual Reports*.

68. David C. Hicks, "Thinking About Organized Crime Prevention," *Journal of Contemporary Criminal Justice* 14.4 (1998): 325–50; CISC, *1999 and 2001 Annual Reports*.

69. CISC, *2001 Annual Report*.

CHAPTER 3

1. Mats Berdal and Monica Serrano, *Transnational Organized Crime and International Security: Business as Usual?* (Boulder, Colo.: Lynne Rienner Publishers, 2002).

2. "International Crime Threat Assessment," *Trends in Organized Crime* 5.4 (2000): 32–144.

3. Chris Eskridge and Brandon Paeper, "The Mexican Cartels: A Challenge for the 21st Century," *Criminal Organizations* 12.1–2 (1998): 5–15.

4. Douglas Keh and Graham Farrell, "Trafficking Drugs in the Global Village," *Transnational Organized Crime* 3.2 (1997): 90–110.

5. 2003 National Drug Control Strategy, 28 February 2003, http://www.whitehouse.gov.

6. Ibid.

7. Phil Williams, "Problems and Dangers Posed by Organized Transnational Crime in the Various Regions of the World," *The United Nations and Transnational Organized Crime*, ed. Phil Williams and Ernesto U. Savona (London: Frank Cass, 1996), 23.

8. Brian Freemantle, *The Octopus: Europe in the Grip of Organized Crime* (London: Orion, 1995); R.T. Naylor, "The Rise of the Modern Arms Black Market and the Fall of Supply-Side Control," *Combating Transnational Crime: Concepts, Activities, and Response*, ed. Phil Williams and Dimitri Vlassis (London: Frank Cass, 1998), 209–36.

9. Graham H. Turbiville, "Weapons Proliferation and Organized Crime: The Russian Military and Security Force Dimension," *Trends in Organized Crime* 3.3 (1997): 18–22.

10. Joseph Albini, R.E. Rogers, Victor Shabalin, Valery Kutushev, Vladimir Moiseev, and Julie Anderson, "Russian Organized Crime: Its History, Structure, and Function," *Journal of Contemporary Criminal Justice* 11.4 (1995): 213–43.

11. "Russia Weapons Cache Unsafe," *Tribune Review* [Pittsburgh], 6 April 2003: A3.

12. "International Crime Threat Assessment," *Trends in Organized Crime* 5.4 (2000): 60–61.

13. International Crime Threat Assessment, 2000.

14. Phil Williams, ed., *Illegal Immigration and Commercial Sex: The New Slave Trade* (London: Frank Cass, 1997); Jonathan M. Winer, "Alien Smuggling: Elements of the Problem and the U.S. Response," *Transnational Organized Crime* 3.1 (1997): 50–58; "Trafficking in Persons Report," *Trends in Organized Crime* 6.2 (2000): 32–43.

15. Livia Pomodoro, "Trafficking and Sexual Exploitation of Women and Children," *Combating Transnational Organized Crime: Concepts, Activities, and Responses,* ed. Phil Williams and Dimitri Vlassis (London: Frank Cass, 1998): 237–42; Tatyana A. Denisova, "Trafficking in Women and Children for Sexual Exploitation," *Trends in Organized Crime* 6.3–4 (2001): 30–36; "Modern Slavery: Trafficking in Women and Children," *Trends in Organized Crime* 3.4 (1998): 3–66; Williams, 1997.

16. Freemantle, 1995.

17. Williams, 1996, 27.

18. Obi N.I. Ebbe, "Slicing Nigeria's National Cake," *Trends in Organized Crime* 4.3 (1999): 29–59.

19. "Organ-Trafficking Eyed in Border Slayings" *Tribune Review* [Pittsburgh], 2 May 2002: A2.

20. Julie Salzano and Stephen W. Hartman, "Cargo Crime," *Transnational*

Organized Crime 3.1 (1998): 39–49; United States, Hearing before the Committee on International Relations, House of Representatives, 104th Congress, 2nd session, *The Threat from Russian Organized Crime* (Washington, D.C.: GPO, 1996); Roslava Resendiz, "International Auto Theft: An Exploratory Research of Organization and Organized Crime on the U.S./Mexico Border," *Criminal Organizations* 12.1–2 (1998): 25–30; Williams, 1996.

21. "The Changing Faces of Organized Crime," *Crime and Justice International* 13.10 (1997): 22.

22. Lauren L. Bernick, "Art and Antiquities Theft," *Transnational Organized Crime* 4.2 (1998): 91–116; Freemantle, 1995.

23. Jayant Abhyankar, "Maritime Fraud and Piracy," *Combating Transnational Organized Crime: Concepts, Activities, and Responses*, ed. Phil Williams and Dimitri Vlassis (London: Frank Cass, 1998), 155–94; "Maritime Crime," *Trends in Organized Crime* 3.4 (1998): 68–108; "International Crime Threat Assessment," 2000.

24. Salzano and Hartman, 1998.

25. "International Crime Threat Assessment," 2000; "Organized Crime and the Environment," *Trends in Organized Crime* 3.2 (1997): 3–9; Jennifer Clapp, "The Illicit Trade in Hazardous Wastes and CFCs: International Responses to Environmental Bads," *Trends in Organized Crime* 3.2 (1997): 14–18.

26. "International Crime Threat Assessment," 2000.

27. Donovan Webster, "The Looting and Smuggling and Fencing and Hoarding of Impossibly Precious, Feathered, and Scaly Wild Things," *Trends in Organized Crime* 3.2 (1997): 9–10; "International Crime Threat Assessment," 2000.

28. "United Nations International Drug Control Programme, World Drug Report," *Trends in Organized Crime* 3.2 (1997): 12–13.

CHAPTER 4

1. Phil Williams, "Money Laundering," *Criminal Organizations* 10.4 (1997): 18.

2. *2002 National Money Laundering Strategy*, 16 March 2003, http://www.whitehouse.gov.

3. Ibid.

4. Ibid.

5. Ibid.

6. Ibid.

7. Ibid.

8. "Special Focus: Fighting Money Laundering: International Trends," *Trends in Organized Crime* 4.4 (1999); Office of Technology Assessment, *Money Laundering: Information Technologies for the Control of Money Laundering* (Washington, D.C.: GPO, 1995); U.S. Department of State, *Money Laundering and Financial Crimes*, (Washington, D.C.: Bureau of International Narcotics and Law Enforcement, 2001); United States, House Committee on Banking and Financial Services, 106th Congress, 2nd Session, *Money Laundering* (Washington, D.C.: GPO, 2000).

9. James R. Richards, *Transnational Criminal Organizations, Cybercrime, and Money Laundering: A Handbook for Law Enforcement Officers, Auditors, and Financial Investigators* (Boca Raton, Fla.: CRC Press, 1999).

10. Linda Gustitus, Elise Bean, and Robert Roach, "Correspondent Banking: A Gateway for Money Laundering," *Economic Perspectives* 6.2 (2001): 26–29, http://www.state.gov; United States, Committee on Governmental Affairs, Permanent Subcommittee on Investigations, 107th Congress, 1st Session, *Report on Correspondent Banking and Money Laundering: A Gateway to Money Laundering* (Washington, D.C.: GPO, 2001).

11. *Money Laundering: Information Technologies for the Control of Money Laundering*, 1995.

12. Richards, 1999; *2002 National Money Laundering Strategy*.

13. Ibid.

14. Richards, 1999; *Money Laundering: Information Technologies for the Control of Money Laundering*, 1995.

15. Richards, 1999, 75–76.

16. Richards, 1999.

17. Ibid.

18. Richards, 1999, 109.

19. Richards, 1999.

20. Lester M. Joseph, "Money Laundering Enforcement: Following the Money," *Economic Perspectives* 6.2 (2001): 11–14, http://www.state.gov.

21. Ibid.

22. *2002 National Money Laundering Strategy*.

23. Lester, 2001.

24. Richards, 1999, 60–61.

25. Lester, 2001.

26. Ibid.

27. "Identity Safeguards Not Up to Task," 30 July 2002, http://www.foxnews.com.

28. "FTC: Identity Theft Nearly Doubled in 2002," 23 January 2003, http://www.foxnews.com.

29. Jeffrey Robinson, *The Merger: How Organized Crime Is Taking Over Canada and the World* (Toronto: McClelland and Stewart, 1999).

30. "H&R Block Tax Customers Become Victims of Identity Theft," 2 January 2003, http://www.foxnews.com.

31. "FBI: Internet Fraud Triples in 2002," 10 April 2003, http://www.foxnews.com.

32. April 2003 update from the International Association for the Study of Organized Crime (IASOC), 30 April 2003, http://www.iasoc.net.

33. P.N. Grabosky, "Crime in Cyberspace," *Combating Transnational Crime: Concepts, Activities, and Responses*, ed. Phil Williams and Dimitri Vlassis (London: Frank Cass, 1998), 195–208.

34. "America's First International Crime Threat Assessment," *Trends in Organized Crime* 5.4 (2000): 32–144.

35. Ibid.

36. Ibid.

37. Gary Potter and Bankole Thompson, "Emerging Influences and Trends in African Organized Crime," *Criminal Organizations* 11.1–2 (1997): 4–9; Obi N. I. Ebbe, "Slicing Nigeria's National Cake," *Trends in Organized Crime* 4.3 (1999): 29–59.

CHAPTER 5

1. Jonathan R. White, *Terrorism: An Introduction*, 2d ed. (Belmont, Calif.: West/Wadsworth, 1998).

2. Brent L. Smith, *Terrorism in America: Pipe Bombs and Pipe Dreams* (Albany: State University of New York Press, 1994); Kenneth S. Stern, *A Force on the Plain: The American Militia Movement and the Politics of Hate* (New York: Simon and Schuster, 1996); Frank Shanty and Raymond Picquet, *Encyclopedia of World Terrorism*, (Armonk, N.Y.: M.E. Sharpe, 2003).

3. Walter Laqueur, *The New Terrorism: Fanaticism and the Arms of Mass Destruction* (New York: Oxford University Press, 1999); Shanty and Picquet, 2003.

4. Laqueur, 1999, 5; Glenn E. Schweitzer and Carole Dorsch Schweitzer, *A Faceless Enemy: the Origins of Modern Terrorism* (Cambridge, Mass.: Oxford, 2002).

5. Laqueur, 1999, 5–6.

6. Frank J. Cilluffo, Sharon L. Cardash, Gordon N. Lederman, *Combating Chemical, Biological, Radiological, and Nuclear Terrorism: A Comprehensive Strategy*, Center for Strategic and International Studies (Washington, D.C.: CSIS Press, 2002).

7. Cilluffo et al., 3–6.

8. Cilluffo et al., 6.

9. Laqueur, 1999.

10. Judith Miller, Stephen Engel, and William Broad, *Germs: Biological Weapons and America's Secret War* (New York: Simon and Schuster, 2001).

11. Laqueur, 1999.

12. Brian Freemantle, *The Octopus: Europe in the Grip of Organized Crime* (London: Orion, 1995).

13. Ibid.

14. Cilluffo et al., 2002.

15. Rensselaer Lee, "Recent Trends in Nuclear Smuggling," *Transnational Organized Crime* 2.4 (1996): 109–21.

16. Joseph Albini, R.E. Rogers, Victor Shabalin, Valery Kutushev, Vladimir Moiseev, and Julie Anderson, "Russian Organized Crime: Its History, Structure, and Function," *Journal of Contemporary Criminal Justice* 11.4 (1995): 213–43.

17. Paul N. Woessner, "Chronology of Radioactive and Nuclear Materials Smuggling Incidents: July 1991–June 1997," *Transnational Organized Crime* 3.1 (1997): 114–209.

18. "Roots of 'Islamic' Terror," *Crime and Justice International* 19.70 (2003): 23.

19. *Crime and Justice International* 18.67 (2002): 29 (Prepared for CJI by the Institute for the Study of Violent Groups).

20. *Crime and Justice International* 19.70 (2003): 29 (Prepared for CJI by the Institute for the Study of Violent Groups).

21. The Terrorism Research Center, 27 April 2003, http://www.homelandsecurity.com; Yonah Alexander and Michael S. Swetnam, *Usama bin Laden's al-Qaida: Profile of a Terrorist Network* (Ardsley, N.Y.: Transnational Publishers, 2001); Paul L. Williams, *Al Qaeda: Brotherhood of Terror* (Parsippany, N.J.: Alpha, 2002).

22. Shanty and Picquet, 2003; Terrorism Research Center, 2003.

23. Greg Rattray, *Strategic Warfare in Cyberspace* (Cambridge, Mass.: MIT Press, 2001).

24. Ibid.

25. Ibid.

26. Rattray, 2001; Mary Dodge, "Slams, Crams, Jams, and Other Phone Scams: Competition, Crime, and Regulation in the Telecommunications Industry," *Journal of Contemporary Criminal Justice* 17.4 (2001): 358–68.

27. Rattray, 2001.

28. Rattray, 2001; Anthony H. Cordesman and Justin G. Cordesman, *Cyberthreats, Information Warfare, and Critical Infrastructure Protection: Defending the U.S. Homeland* (Westport, Conn.: Praeger, 2002); P.N. Grabosky, "Crime in Cyberspace," *Transnational Organized Crime*, 4.3–4 (1998): 195–208.

29. Rattray, 2001; Cordesman and Cordesman, 2002.

30. *2002 National Money Laundering Strategy*.

CHAPTER 6

1. Emilio C. Viano, *Global Organized Crime and International Security* (Bookfield, Vt.: Ashgate, 1999); James B. Jacobs, Christopher Panarella, and Jay Worthington, *Busting the Mob: U.S. vs. Cosa Nostra* (New York: New York University Press, 1994); Patrick J. Ryan, *Organized Crime: A Reference Handbook* (Santa Barbara, Calif.: ABC-CLIO, Inc., 1995).

2. Michael Lyman and Gary W. Potter, *Organized Crime*, 2d ed. (Upper Saddle River, N.J.: Prentice-Hall, 2000); G. Robert Blakey, "Asset Forfeiture Under the Federal Criminal Law," *The Politics and Economics of Organized Crime*, ed. Herbert E. Alexander and Gerald E. Caiden (Toronto: D.C. Heath and Company, 1985).

3. *Information Technologies for the Control of Money Laundering* (Washington, D.C.: Office of Technology Assessment, 1995).

4. *2003 National Drug Control Strategy*, http://www.whitehouse.gov.

5. Ibid.

6. Office of Technology Assessment, 1995; "Fighting Money Laundering: International Trends," *Trends in Organized Crime* 4.4 (1999).

7. Phil Williams, "Money Laundering," *Criminal Organizations* 10.4 (1997): 18.

8. *Information Technologies for the Control of Money Laundering*, 1995.

9. Christopher Doyle, "The USA Patriot Act: A Sketch," a Congressional Research Service (CRS) Report for Congress (2002).

10. Office of Technology Assessment, 1995.

11. Ibid.

12. "The Fight Against Money Laundering," *Economic Perspectives* 6.2 (2001), http://www.state.gov.

13. *2002 National Money Laundering Strategy*, http://www.whitehouse.gov.

14. Ibid.

15. Ibid.

16. Ibid.

17. "Seaports Begin Using Electronic Container Security System," *Tribune Review* [Pittsburgh], 18 January 2003: A5.

18. "Ashcroft, Canadian Leaders Hail Agreement to Bolster Border Security," 3 December 2001, http://www.cnn.com.

19. "INS Wants Details on Those Traveling in or out of the U.S.," 4 January 2003, http://www.cnn.com.; "ACLU Calls Immigrant Registration Program Pretext for Mass Detentions," 19 December 2002, http://www.ACLU.org.

20. *Tribune Review*, 18 January 2003.

21. "Law Enforcement in 'Real Time,'" *Crime and Justice International* 18.68 (2002): 32.

22. Ralph De Palma, "Satellite-Based Cargo Container Intrusion Monitoring and Reporting System," *Trends in Organized Crime* 3.4 (1998): 107–8.

23. *Tribune Review*, 18 January 2003.

24. Daniel Mabrey, "Biometrics: The New Face of Border Security," *Crime and Justice International* 18.68 (2002): 31–32; "Irises, Voices Give Away Terrorists," 7 November 2002, http://www.cnn.com.; "Walk the Walk..." *Crime and Justice International* 19.71 (2003): 32.

25. Kim Zetter, "Tracing Terrorists the Las Vegas Way," 7 August 2002, http://www.PCWorld.com.

26. Mabrey, 2002.

27. Erin Hayes, "Detecting Terror: Lab Develops New Ways to Identify and Fight Terrorist Attacks," 16 December 2002, http://www.abcnews.com.

28. *EFF Analysis of the Provisions of the USA Patriot Act that Relate to Online Activities*, 31 October 2001, http://www.eff.org.; Doyle, 2002.

29. Ibid.

30. *2002 National Money Laundering Strategy.*

31. EFF Analysis, 2001; Doyle, 2002.

32. Ibid.

33. "Case Against Florida Professor Tests New Federal Powers," *Tribune Review* [Pittsburgh], 26 February 2003: A11.

34. "Americans May be Held as 'Enemy Combatants,' Appeals Court Rules," 8 January 2003, http://www.cnn.com.

35. Michael Scardaville, "No Orwellian Scheme Behind DARPA's Total Information Awareness System," 20 November 2002, http://www.heritage.org.

36. "The Backdoor, the Hidden Agent, and the Mishap: The Hidden Dangers of Carnivore," 10 March 2003, http://www.stopcarnivore.org; "Carnivore Diagnostic Tool," 10 March 2003, http://www.fbi.gov.

37. Michael Scardaville, "The Homeland Security Act of 2002: An Analysis," 24 July 2003, http://www.heritage.org.

38. "Study Faults INS for Lax Security," Gannett News Service, 24 January 2003.

39. Ibid.

40. "The Border War: Our Losing Battle," *Tribune Review* [Pittsburgh], 8 February 2003: A8.

41. "FBI Director: About 100 Attacks Thwarted," 14 December 2002, http://www.cnn.com.

42. Gregory J. Rattray, *Strategic Warfare in Cyberspace* (Cambridge, Mass.: MIT Press, 2001); Anthony H. Cordesman with Justin G. Cordesman, *Cyber-threats, Information Warfare, and Critical Infrastructure Protection: Defending the U.S. Homeland* (Westport, Conn.: Praeger, 2002).

43. Rattray, 2001; Cordesman, 2002.

44. Ibid.

45. Ibid.

46. Dorothy E. Denning and William E. Baugh, "Encryption and Evolving Technologies: Tools of Organized Crime and Terrorism," *Trends in Organized Crime* 3.3 (1998): 44–75.

47. Ted Bridis, "FBI Is Building 'Magic Lantern,'" 23 November 2001, Associated Press.

48. "The United States International Crime Control Strategy," *Trends in Organized Crime* 4.1 (1998).

49. "The Palermo Convention on Transnational Crime," *Trends in Organized Crime* 5.4 (2000).

50. Raymond E. Kendall, "Responding to Transnational Crime," *Combating Transnational Crime: Concepts, Activities, and Responses,* ed. Phil Williams and Dimitri Vlassis (London: Frank Cass, 1999), 269–75; Paul Swallow, "Of Limited Operational Relevance: A European View of Interpol's Crime-Fighting Role in the Twenty-First Century," *Transnational Organized Crime* 2.4 (1996): 106–30.

51. *The Rome Statute of the International Criminal Court,* http://www.un.org.

CHAPTER 7

1. Peter Andreas, "Transnational Crime and Economic Globalization," ed. Mats Berdal and Monica Serrano, *Transnational Organized Crime and International Security: Business as Usual?* (Boulder, Colo.: Lynne Rienner Publishers, 2002), 37–52; Michael Levi, "Liberalization and Transnational Financial Crime," ed. Mats Berdal and Monica Serrano, *Transnational Organized Crime and International Security: Business as Usual?* (Boulder, Colo.: Lynne Rienner Publishers, 2002), 53–66.

2. "The United States International Crime Control Strategy," *Trends in Organized Crime* 4.1 (1998).

3. "America's First International Crime Threat Assessment," *Trends in Organized Crime* 5.4 (2000): 32–144.

Selected Bibliography

Abadinsky, Howard. *Organized Crime*. 6th ed. Chicago: Nelson-Hall, 2000.

Abhyankar, Jayant. "Maritime Fraud and Piracy." *Combating Transnational Organized Crime: Concepts, Activities, and Responses.* Special issue of *Transnational Organized Crime* 4.3–4 (1998): 155–94.

"ACLU Calls Immigrant Registration Program Pretext for Mass Detentions." 19 December 2002. http://www.aclu.org.

Albanese, Jay. *Organized Crime in America*. 3rd ed. Cincinnatti: Anderson, 1996.

Albini, Joseph. *The American Mafia: Genesis of a Legend*. New York: Appleton-Century Crofts, 1971.

Albini, Joseph, R.E. Rogers, Victor Shabalin, Valery Kutushev, Vladimir Moiseev, and Julie Anderson. "Russian Organized Crime: Its History, Structure, and Function." *Journal of Contemporary Criminal Justice* 11.4 (1995): 213–43.

Alexander, Yonah, and Michael S. Swetnam. *Usama bin Laden's al-Qaida: Profile of a Terrorist Network*. New York: Transnational Publishers, 2001.

"America's First International Crime Threat Assessment." *Trends in Organized Crime*. Summer 2000: 32–144.

Arlachi, Pino. *Mafia Business: The Mafia Ethic and the Spirit of Capitalism*. New York: Verso, 1987.

"Ashcroft, Canadian Leaders Hail Agreement to Bolster Border Security." 3 December 2001. http://www.cnn.com.

"The Backdoor, the Hidden Agent, and the Mishap: The Hidden Dangers of Carnivore." 10 June 2003. http://www.stopcarnivore.org.

Beare, M.E. *Criminal Conspiracies: Organized Crime in America*. Toronto: Nelson, 1996.

Behan, Tom. *The Camorra*. New York: Routledge, 1995.

Berdal, Mats, and Monica Serrano. *Transnational Organized Crime and Interna-*

tional Security: Business as Usual? Boulder, Colo.: Lynne Rienner Publishers, 2002.

Bernick, Lauren L. "Art and Antiquities Theft." *Transnational Organized Crime* 4.2 (1995): 91–116.

Block, Alan A. *East Side-West Side: Organizing Crime in New York, 1930–1950.* New Brunswick, N.J.: Transaction, 1983.

Booth, Martin. *The Triads: The Chinese Criminal Fraternity.* London: Grafton, 1990.

"The Border War: Our Losing Battle." *Tribune Review* [Pittsburgh], 8 February 2003: A8.

Bray, Marianne. "Foreign Triads Infiltrating China." 18 March 2002. http://www.cnn.com.

Bridis, Ted. "FBI Is Building 'Magic Lantern.'" 23 November 2001. Associated Press.

"Brothers Guilty in Charlotte Terror Trial." 25 June 2002. http://www.cnn.com.

Bunker, Robert J., and John P. Sullivan. "Cartel Evolution: Potentials and Consequences." *Transnational Organized Crime* 4.2 (1998): 55–74.

Burlingame, Timothy M. "Criminal Activity in the Russian Banking System." *Transnational Organized Crime* 3.3 (1997): 46–72.

"Bust May Mark End of Drug Kingpin Era." *Tribune Review* [Pittsburgh], 16 March 2003: A2.

"Carnivore Diagnostic Tool." 23 May 2003. http://www.fbi.gov.

"Case against Florida professor tests new federal powers." *Tribune Review* [Pittsburgh], 26 February 2003: A11.

"The Changing Faces of Organized Crime." *Crime and Justice International: Worldwide News and Trends* 13.10 (1997): 22.

"Child Smuggling Ring Broken, INS Says." 12 August 2002. http://www.cnn.com.

Cilluffo, Frank J., Sharon L. Cardash, and Gordon N. Lederman. *Combating Chemical, Biological, Radiological, and Nuclear Terrorism: A Comprehensive Strategy.* Washington, D.C.: Center for Strategic and International Studies, CSIS Press, 2002.

Clapp, Jennifer. "The Illicit Trade in Hazardous Wastes and CFCs: International Responses to Environmental Bads." *Trends in Organized Crime* 3.2 (1997): 14–18.

Cordesman, Anthony H., and Justin G. Cordesman. *Cyber-threats, Information Warfare, and Critical Infrastructure Protection: Defending the U.S. Homeland.* Westport, Conn.: Praeger, 2002.

Craig, Mark. "Best Practice in Intelligence Management with Respect to Chinese Organized Crime." *Trends in Organized Crime* 3.2 (1997): 62–66.

Criminal Intelligence Service Canada. *1996 Annual Report.*

———. *1997 Annual Report.*

———. *1998 Annual Report.*

———. *1999 Annual Report.*

———. *2000 Annual Report.*

———. *2001 Annual Report.*

———. *2002 Annual Report.*

Denisova, Tatyana A. "Trafficking in Women and Children for Sexual Exploitation." *Trends in Organized Crime* 6.3–4 (2001): 30–36.

Denning, Dorothy E., and William E. Baugh. "Encryption and Evolving Technologies: Tools of Organized Crime and Terrorism." U.S. Working Group on Organized Crime, National Strategy Information Center. *Trends in Organized Crime* 3.3 (1998): 44–75.

De Palma, Ralph. "Satellite-Based Cargo Container Intrusion Monitoring and Reporting System." *Trends in Organized Crime* 3.4 (1998): 107–8.

Department of the Solicitor General, Canada. "Organized Crime Impact Study." 22 July 2002. http://www.sgc.gc.ca\Efact\eorgcrime.htm.

EFF Analysis of the Provisions of the USA Patriot Act that Relate to Online Activities. 31 October 2001. http://www.eff.org.

Eskridge, Chris and Brandon Paeper. "The Mexican Cartels: A Challenge for the 21st Century." *Criminal Organizations* 12.1–2 (1998): 5–15.

"FBI: Internet Fraud Triples in 2002." 10 April 2003. http://www.foxnews.com.

"FBI Director: About 100 Attacks Thwarted." 14 December 2002. http://www.cnn.com.

"The FBI Perspective" [on organized crime in the U.S.]. *Crime and Justice International* 19.72 (2003): 13–16.

"The Fight Against Money Laundering." *Economic Perspectives* 6.2. May 2001. http://www.state.gov.

"Fighting Money Laundering: International Trends." *Trends in Organized Crime* 4.4 (1999).

Finckenauer, James O., and Yuri Voronin. *The Threat of Russian Organized Crime.* Washington: National Institute of Justice, 2001.

Foglesong, Todd S., and Peter Solomon, Jr. *Crime, Criminal Justice, and Criminology in Post-Soviet Ukraine.* Washington, D.C.: National Institute of Justice, 2001.

Freemantle, Brian. *The Octopus: Europe in the Grip of Organized Crime.* London: Orion, 1995.

"FTC: Identity Theft Nearly Doubled in 2002." 23 January 2003. http://www.foxnews.com.

"Gangs Net Millions from Software Piracy." 6 May 1999. http://www.cnn.com.

Grabosky, P.N. "Crime in Cyberspace." *Transnational Organized Crime* 4.3–4 (1998): 195–208.

Gustitus, Linda, Elise Bean, and Robert Roach. "Correspondent Banking: A Gateway for Money Laundering." *Economic Perspectives* 6.2 (2001): 26–29. http://www.state.gov.

"H&R Block Tax Customers Become Victims of Identity Theft." 2 January 2003. http://www.foxnews.com.

Hayes, Erin. "Detecting Terror: Lab Develops New Ways to Identify and Fight Terrorist Attacks." 16 December 2002. http://www.abcnews.com.

Hicks, David C. "Thinking About Organized Crime Prevention," *Journal of Contemporary Criminal Justice.* 14.4 (1998): 325–50.

The Homeland Security Act of 2002. H.R. 5005. http://www.house.gov.

"Identity Safeguards Not Up to Task." 30 July 2002. http://www.foxnews.com.

Information Technologies for the Control of Money Laundering. Washington: Office of Technology Assessment, 1995.

"INS Wants Details on Those Traveling in or out of the U.S." 4 January 2003. http://www.cnn.com.

"International Crime Control Strategy." *Trends in Organized Crime* 4.1 (1998).

"International Crime Threat Assessment." *Trends in Organized Crime* 5.4 (2000): 32–144.

"Irises, voices give away terrorists." 7 November 2003. http://www.cnn.com.

Jacobs, James B., Christopher Panarella, and Jay Worthington. *Busting the Mob: U.S. v. Cosa Nostra.* New York: New York University Press, 1994.

Joseph, Lester M. "Money Laundering Enforcement: Following the Money." *Economic Perspectives* 6.2 (2001): 11–14.

Keh, Douglas, and Graham Farrell. "Trafficking Drugs in the Global Village." *Transnational Organized Crime* 3.2 (1997): 90–110.

Kendall, Raymond E. "Responding to Transnational Crime." *Combating Transnational Crime: Concepts, Activities, and Responses.* Edited by Phil Williams and Dimitri Vlassis. Special issue of *Transnational Organized Crime* 4.3–4 (1998): 269–75.

Kuzio, Taras. "Crime Still Ukraine's Greatest Enemy." *Trends in Organized Crime* 3.1 (1997): 27–30.

Laqueur, Walter. *The New Terrorism: Fanaticism and the Arms of Mass Destruction.* New York: Oxford University Press, 1999.

"Law Enforcement in 'Real Time.'" *Crime and Justice International* 18.68 (2002): 32.

Lee, Rensselaer. "Recent Trends in Nuclear Smuggling." *Transnational Organized Crime* 2.4 (1996): 109–21.

Lupsha, Peter. "Transnational Organized Crime Versus the Nation State." *Transnational Organized Crime* 2.1 (1996): 21–48.

Mabrey, Daniel. "Biometrics: The New Face of Border Security." *Crime and Justice International* 18.68 (2002): 31–32.

"Maritime Crime." *Trends in Organized Crime* 3.4 (1998): 68–108.

"Mexican Police Arrest Suspected Drug Kingpin." 10 March 2002. http://www.cnn.com.

Miller, Judith, Stephen Engel, and William Broad. *Germs: Biological Weapons and America's Secret War.* New York: Simon and Schuster, 2001.

"Modern Slavery: Trafficking in Women and Children." *Trends in Organized Crime* 3.4 (1998): 3–66.

Money Laundering: Information Technologies for the Control of Money Laundering. Office of Technology Assessment. Washington, D.C.: GPO, 1995.

Money Laundering and Financial Crimes. U.S. Department of State, Washington, D.C.: Bureau of International Narcotics and Law Enforcement, 2001.

"More Mafia Indictments in New York." 6 September 2002 http://www.cnn.com.

Mueller, Gerhard, O.W. "Transnational Crime: Definitions and Concepts." *Transnational Organized Crime* 4.3–4 (1998): 13–21.

"Music Chiefs Warn of Piracy Threat." 21 January 2001. http://www.cnn.com.

"National Drug Control Strategy." 15 May 2003. http://www.whitehouse.gov.

"National Money Laundering Strategy." 30 May 2003. http://www.whitehouse.gov.

Naylor, R.T. "The Rise of the Modern Arms Black Market and the Fall of Supply-Side Control." *Transnational Organized Crime* 4.3–4 (1998): 209–36.

"Nearly 8,000 Arrested in Alien Smuggling Scheme." 27 June 2001. http://www.cnn.com.

Nieves, Robert J. "Breaking Drug Cartels: Lessons from Colombia." *Trends in Organized Crime* 3.3 (1998)13–29.

Organized Crime Agency of British Columbia. *2001 Annual Report.*

"Organized Crime and the Environment." *Trends in Organized Crime* 3.2 (1997): 3–9.

"Organ-Trafficking Eyed in Border Slayings." *Tribune Review* [Pittsburgh], 2 May 2002: A2.

"The Palermo Convention on Transnational Crime." *Trends in Organized Crime* 5.4 (2000).

Palmer, Richard L. "The New Russian Oligarchy: The Nomenklatura, the KGB, and the Mafiya." *Trends in Organized Crime* 3.1 (1997): 8–14.

"Patterns of Global Terrorism, 2001." 15 October 2002. http://www.state.gov.

Pimentel, Stanley A. "Mexico's Legacy of Corruption." *Trends in Organized Crime* 4.3 (1999): 9–28.

"Police Say Suspect Confesses to Bali Bombing." 22 November 2002. http://www.cnn.com.

Pomodoro, Livia. "Trafficking and Sexual Exploitation of Women and Children." *Transnational Organized Crime* 4.3–4 (1998): 237–42.

Potter, Gary, and Bankole Thompson. "Emerging Influences and Trends in African Organized Crime." *Criminal Organizations* 11.1–2 (1997): 4–9.

Rattray, Greg. *Strategic Warfare in Cyberspace.* Cambridge, Mass.: MIT Press, 2001.

Resendiz, Roslava. "International Auto Theft: An Exploratory Research of Organization and Organized Crime on the U.S./Mexico Border." *Criminal Organizations* 12.1–2 (1998): 25–30.

Richard, Mark M., Michael C. Stenger, and Jonathan Winer. Prepared statements before the Subcommittee on Africa of the House International Relations Committee. *Trends in Organized Crime* 3.2 (1997): 131–49.

Richards, James R. *Transnational Criminal Organizations, Cybercrime, and Money Laundering: A Handbook for Law Enforcement Officers, Auditors, and Financial Investigators.* Boca Raton, Fla.: CRC Press, 1999.

The Rome Statute of the International Criminal Court. 15 March 2003. http://
    www.un.org.

"Roots of 'Islamic' Terror." *Crime and Justice International* 19.70 (2003): 23.

"Russia Weapons Cache Unsafe." *Tribune Review* [Pittsburgh], 6 April 2003: A3.

"Russian Money Laundering Probe Widens as First Charges Filed." 6 October 1999.
    http://www.cnn.com.

"Russian Organized Crime Implicated in Figure Skating Scandal." 21 August 2002.
    http://www.cnn.com.

Salzano, Julie, and Stephen W. Hartman. "Cargo Crime." *Transnational Organized
    Crime* 3.1 (1997): 39–49.

Scardaville, Michael. "The Homeland Security Act of 2002: An Analysis." 24 July
    2002. http://www.Heritage.org.

———. "No Orwellian Scheme Behind DARPA's Total Information Awareness Sys-
    tem." 20 November 2002. http://www.Heritage.org.

Schmid, Alex P. "Links between Transnational Organized Crime and Terrorist
    Crimes." *Transnational Organized Crime* 2.4 (1996): 41–81.

Schneider, Stephen R. "Combating Organized Crime in (and by) the Private Sector:
    A Normative Role for Canada's Forensic Investigative Firms." *Journal of
    Contemporary Criminal Justice* 14.4 (1998): 351–67.

Schweitzer, Glenn E., and Carole Dorsch Schweitzer. *A Faceless Enemy: the Origins
    of Modern Terrorism.* Cambridge, Mass.: Oxford University Press, 2002.

"Seaports Begin Using Electronic Container Security System." *Tribune Review* [Pitts-
    burgh], 18 January 2003: A5.

Shanty, Frank, and Raymond Picquet. *Encyclopedia of World Terrorism.* New York:
    M.E. Sharpe, 2003.

Shelley, Louise I. "The Price Tag of Russia's Organized Crime." *Trends in Orga-
    nized Crime* 3.1 (1997): 24–26.

"Special Focus: Fighting Money Laundering: International Trends." *Trends in Or-
    ganized Crime* 4.4 (1999).

Stenger, Richard. "Report: Russian Mob Threatens Prime Fishery." 12 December
    2001. http://www.cnn.com.

"Study Faults INS for Lax Security." *Gannett News Service.* 24 January 2003.

Swallow, Paul. "Of Limited Operational Relevance: A European View of Interpol's
    Crime-Fighting Role in the Twenty-First Century." *Transnational Organized
    Crime* 2.4 (1996): 106–30.

"Trafficking in Persons Report." *Trends in Organized Crime* 6.2 (2000): 32–43.

Turbiville, Graham H. "Weapons Proliferation and Organized Crime: The Russian
    Military and Security Force Dimension." *Trends in Organized Crime* 3.3
    (1997): 18–22.

Ulrich, Christopher J., and Timo A. Kivimaki. *Uncertain Security: Confronting
    Transnational Crime in the Baltic Sea Region and Russia.* Lanham, Md.:
    Lexington Books, 2002.

"U.N.: Child Sex Trade a Form of Terrorism." 17 December 2001. http://
    www.cnn.com.

"United Nations International Drug Control Programme, World Drug Report." *Trends in Organized Crime* 3.2 (1997) 12–13.

United States Congress. House. Committee on International Relations. *Global Organized Crime.* 104th Congress, 2nd session. Washington, D.C.: GPO, 1996.

———. House. Committee on Banking and Financial Services. *Money Laundering.* 106th Congress, 2nd session. Washington, D.C.: GPO, 2000.

———. House. Subcommittee on Crime of the Committee on the Judiciary. *Drug Trafficking on the Southwest Border.* 107th Congress, 1st session. Washington, D.C.: GPO, 29 March 2001.

———. Senate. Committee on Governmental Affairs, Permanent Subcommittee on Investigations. *Report on Correspondent Banking and Money Laundering: A Gateway to Money Laundering.* 107th Congress, 1st session. Washington, D.C.: GPO, 2001.

"The United States International Crime Control Strategy." *Trends in Organized Crime* 4.1 (1998).

"U.S. Infrastructure Information Found on Al-Qaida Computers." 27 June 2002. http://www.cnn.com.

"U.S. Prosecutors File Charges Against Members of Colombian Rebel Group." 13 November 2002. http://www.cnn.com.

Viano, Emilio C. *Global Organized Crime and International Security.* Bookfield, Vt.: Ashgate, 1999.

"Walk the Walk..." *Crime and Justice International* 19.71 (2003): 32.

Webster, Donovan. "The Looting and Smuggling and Fencing and Hoarding of Impossibly Precious, Feathered, and Scaly Wild Things." *Trends in Organized Crime* 3.2 (1997): 9–10.

Webster, William H., Arnaud de Borchgrave, and Frank J. Cilluffo. *Russian Organized Crime: Putin's Challenge.* Global Organized Crime Project. Washington: Center for Strategic and International Studies, 2000.

White, Jonathan R. *Terrorism: An Introduction,* 2d ed. Belmont, Calif.: West/ Wadsworth, 1998.

Williams, Paul L. *Al Qaeda: Brotherhood of Terror.* Parsippany, N.J.: Alpha, 2002.

Williams, Phil. "Cooperation Among Criminal Organizations." *Transnational Organized Crime and International Security.* Edited by Mats Berdal and Monica Serrano. Boulder, Colo.: Lynne Rienner Publishers, 2002.

———, ed. "Illegal Migration and Commercial Sex: The New Slave Trade." *Transnational Organized Crime* 3.4 (1997).

———. "Money Laundering." *Criminal Organizations* 10.4 (1997): 18–27.

———, ed. *Russian Organized Crime.* London: Frank Cass, 1997.

Winer, Jonathan M. "Alien Smuggling: Elements of the Problem and the U.S. Response." *Transnational Organized Crime* 3.1 (1997): 50–58.

Woessner, Paul N. "Chronology of Radioactive and Nuclear Materials Smuggling Incidents: July 1991–June 1997." *Transnational Organized Crime* 3.1 (1997): 114–209.

Wo-Lap Lam, Willy. "China Corruption Linked to Triads." 10 March 2002.
    http://www.cnn.com.
Zabludoff, Sidney J. "Colombian Narcotics Organizations as Business Enterprises."
    Transnational Organized Crime 3.2 (1997): 20–49.
Zetter, Kim. "Tracing Terrorists the Las Vegas Way." 7 August 2002. http://
    www.PCWorld.com.

Index

About the Author

DONALD R. LIDDICK JR. is Associate Professor of Administration of Justice at the University of Pittsburgh, Greensburg. He has published three books and several articles that have appeared in various journals.